NFL-AFL
FOOTBALL
GUIDE
1968

NFL-AFL FOOTBALL GUIDE 1968

FRANK GIFFORD

CBS Sports Broadcaster

An NAL book distributed jointly by
The New American Library
and The World Publishing Company

First printing

Published by The New American Library, Inc.
1301 Avenue of the Americas, New York, New York, 10019

Library of Congress Catalog Card Number: 68-55652

Printed in the United States of America

DEDICATED TO ALL THE CENTERS,
GUARDS, AND TACKLES, WHO DO ALL THE WORK,
GET ALL THE HEADACHES,
AND READ ABOUT ALL THE "HEROES."

CONTENTS

PREFACE

Professional football is proud of Frank Gifford.
He was one of the finest of its players, and what
he contributed to the game and what he gained
from it are both clearly evident in this book.

PETE ROZELLE
Commissioner

INTRODUCTION

For twenty years, the game of football was my life, my love, and my dedication.

It began on the sandlots of Bakersfield, California, and wound up in Yankee Stadium, with stop-offs at Bakersfield High School and Junior College and the University of Southern California.

My first football was a flour sack filled with rags . . . my last an official NFL "Duke," the one I dropped against Cleveland in the fourth quarter of the last game in which I played. My first uniform was a pair of torn "Levis" . . . my last, the lightweight red and blue of the New York Giants.

Still, in looking back, as all ex-athletes tend to do, I find it hard for me to distinguish between the Frank Gifford of the sandlots and the Frank Gifford of the Giants. Most certainly there was the natural physical development that came with age and maturity, but inside, where one "lives," my approach to the game remained pretty much the same. I like to think my attitude toward football was much the same as that of professional players today, and it's something which I've considered often in preparing for and telecasting games.

Surely the game has changed, as it does each and every year. The players today are more skillful than they were a year ago and, make no mistake about it, they'll be better next year and even better the following year. That's how it is and the nonsensical recollections of the "ole timers" living in the past are to me a big bore.

The economics of today's game are also vastly different than those of a few years ago, and they are changing constantly. The phenomenal acceptance of the game has brought affluence to the players, and headaches and wealth to the owners. But through all the changes, the one remaining constant has been the basic makeup of the men who play the game.

Nearly all of them are products of the "street," from families of modest or less than modest economic means. As youngsters in the grade and high schools, they found through football the recognition their less than affluent environment could not give them. Their skills on the field opened doors, initially, to a "place" in the campus society. Later, with more maturity, they recognized that their passing arm, their sure tackling ability, their speed, their coordination could also serve as economic stepping stones. More simply put, the best players are the "hungry" players, hungry for success, recognition, and economic rewards.

They are also collectively the greatest "guys" in the world. For 12 years as a New York Giant, I was fortunate enough to belong to their fraternity. I say "was" because that's how it is. Once you leave the game, you no longer really belong, regardless of your record. Even the players who are forced to sit out games with injuries recognize this. They are not ostracized, nor ignored. It's just not the same when you're not contributing to the over-all effort.

You can call it what you like, *esprit de corps,* togetherness, teamwork, but whatever the label, every top pro team has it. Jerry Kramer, the Green Bay Packers great offensive guard, in a post-championship-game inter-view last season, perhaps said it the best. Before a television audience of millions, Jerry unashamedly stated, "We love each other. It's like living in Camelot. We have no stars, only Packers."

What Jerry said made a lot of sense to me. I had known that same feel-ing throughout my years with the Giants. It enabled us to win champion-ships and titles, when on paper we should have never been in the play-offs.

This "oneness" is a by-product of the game of football, and the game of football is not always as it appears. The color and pageantry you see and feel on "game" day in a jam-packed stadium is only a superficial reflection of the real thing.

Unlike other professional sports, when a new football season begins, past records mean little or nothing. Each and every pro regardless of star status must go through the drudgery of a hot and sometimes almost inhu-man summer training camp. In these 26 camps scattered across the nation, there are no bands, no cheering thousands, no television cameras, It's real, and the age-old saying, "Where the men are separated from the boys," comes to life.

Here the fears and doubts are as real as the fatiguing conditioning and brutal contact. The fears are not of the pain that might come with a sud-den, unexpected injury, but rather what that injury might do to your chances of earning one of the 40 positions on a team. The doubts are of one's own ability.

The first day of training camp is always the same. You walk on to the train-ing field and see as many as 100 players. Your mathematics are good . . . 40 from 100 is 60 . . . and that's how many of those individuals are going to fall by the wayside before opening day. During the course of the next two months they disappear almost mysteriously. Some leave in the middle of a sleepless night, after arriving at man's toughest decision, "I'm just not good enough." Others, driven by pride and desperation, push muscle, bone, and ligament beyond its strength. These players leave with the minimal satisfaction of thinking that had they not come up with that knee, ankle, shoulder, or muscle pull, they would have made it.

However they go, they always do. And then it's the middle of September and again you look around and the chosen 40 remain. There's seldom a thought of those who have gone. The season is at hand, and you are 14 games and 35 hours of combat away from a title.

Here is where a team becomes "one." Nothing is as important as the unit. Coaches, wives, sweethearts, friends all circulate on the fringe. The individ-ual's fears and doubts are still with him, only now, in contrast to training camp, where each man is alone, he has the strength of others.

12

Now it's game day. You trot on to the field and the noise of the packed stadium, the smell and the feel of thousands, is almost frightening. Your uniform is new. It's uncomfortable. Your new shoes are laced too tight, or too loose.

You line up for warm-up drills, and you do it as casually and cockily as you can. You don't really feel it, but at the other end of the field there are 40 other "guys" who you hope like hell are unable to read any of your inner feelings.

You drift down field under a "strange" new football thrown by your quarterback. It takes you into the "enemy's" warm-up area, and there "he" is. He might be the man who is going to cover you for the next two and a half hours. If you're a guard or tackle, he'll be the man you're going to try and crush, play after play.

You've studied him all week on film. Now you give him a casual glance, and invariably he's looking just as casually at you. You think, "God, he's big," or "Jeez, he didn't look that quick on film." More often than not, you know him personally from All-Star games, off-season golf tournaments, or from games played in previous years. You might even nod, go out of your way to shake his hand, or pat him on the fanny.

It's gamesmanship, and in an emotional game like football, how you play your role is vitally important. Off the field and back in the locker room, you have 20 minutes to finalize your preparations. Each individual has his own little ritual. The offensive linemen are together, adjusting pads that are already adjusted, while they quietly discuss plays designed for today's game plan.

The big defensive tackles and ends add tape to hands that in a few minutes will be striking, pulling, and pushing other big men.

The receivers discuss pass cuts. The quarterbacks talk in low tones with the offensive coach and the trainers move quickly around, applying "eye black."

The tension builds to where you could almost cut it with a knife. Never has 20 minutes gone so slowly. You want it to pass, and, in a way, you don't. Finally, the "head man" is standing in front of the door. Like the players, he's very quiet. He looks almost ridiculous, and most certainly out of place. He is a professional coach, and because of it he knows that it's all "in." He's done all he can, and while he looks confidently about the room, you know he has as many doubts as you.

"All right, everybody up," and his voice is the first real sound you've heard for those long 20 minutes. Forty men now edge to the door. The coach, no matter how large, becomes lost surrounded by huge men in big pads. He doesn't say much, and if he did you wouldn't hear.

Then the door is opened and you're on your way through a damp smelly tunnel to the field. It's tight and it's cramped as you exit into the dugout, where again you feel the crowd. You look across the way and you see the big bodies of the "enemy" standing and waiting in their dugout. You're in the greatest shape of your life, yet you feel weak. It's a heady, exhilarating feeling that can only be known from experience.

The P.A. announcer breaks the buzz of the fans. "Introducing the starting line-up. . . ," and one by one, to cheers for the home team and boos for the "enemy," the two elevens who'll start the afternoon's battle trot on-to the field.

On the sidelines, now only moments away from kickoff, there's the ritual of the huddle. Many have a special prayer. Others just crowd close. The coin has been tossed a half hour ago, but the traditional ceremony is now being concluded at center field.

Your legs are no longer weak. You're part of 40 men who'll collectively dedicate all their efforts for the next two and one half hours to one thing, a victory. Your first shocking contact on the field empties your stomach of any and all remaining "butterflies."

Then in the huddle, and now more mentally alert than seemingly is humanly possible, you listen to your quarterback capsule into a few numerical comments months of preparation. A third and short yardage might call for a 34-slant from a flanker-right formation . . . a simple play on the blackboard during the week, it is now complicated by an enemy tackle across the line who isn't the "pigeon" he appeared to be during the previous week's study of game films.

Before the call is completed — formation, snap number, etc., — you can hear the linemen quietly plotting adjustments. The tackle and the guard, at the point of the attack, switch assignments with code colors or numbers — and sometimes, if they've been together long enough, they can make the adjustments with a mere gesture or glance.

Leaving the huddle, the 250-pound tackle who's been taking the beating from the aroused "pigeon" might offer some advice to the back who's drawn the running assignment. "Hit it wider," or "Hit it quicker" . . . or if the tackle knows it's going to be rougher than the last time, he might even smile and tell the back, "Hang on to your hat."

Meanwhile, across the neutral zone, the defensive quarterback has also sized up the situation — yardage needed, time remaining, score, tempo of the game. This one small battle in the overall war might call for a "four-three outside blitz Wanda."

The call is made, the defensive huddle broken, and here the quick professional adjustments are made in the assignments that flow so easily onto a blackboard in the form of X's and O's.

"Wanda" is the weak-side linebacker. He'll be red-dogging. He needs help from the end on his side. The middle linebacker in the "four-big-man — three-linebacker setup" that's been called wants his tackle to close down on "that" guard who's been "killing me all afternoon."

They're there . . . nose to nose on the line . . . eyeball to eyeball in the secondary and backfield.

The quarterback looks over a readied defense and makes the final decision. "Shall I go through with it, or should I change it?" With one "live" color or number, he can change the entire play if he deems it necessary. Each offensive man waits for his first sound. If it's a "dummy number" the play remains as called. If it's the "live" number. . . ? But then, there it is, the dummy call. We're going through with the 34-slant. The count comes — the ball is popped up, and it either happens or it doesn't in an explosive three or four seconds.

Each skirmish in the overall battle is like this. The result is either satisfaction or frustration.

In an afternoon there are approximately 150 such happenings, and then it's over. Your hurts and bruises, aches and pains are in direct proportion to the outcome of the game. If you've won, and have made your contribution, the satisfaction deep inside is both a feeling of pride as an individual, and pride in belonging to a group whose efforts have met the challenge. If you've lost, you hide the despair that accompanies failure, and live with the thoughts of "If I'd only . . ." or "Dammit, why didn't I?" It'll happen in over 200 games this fall, with each team and each individual contributing his share to the six-months season.

In the ensuing chapters, it'll be my aim to make that season and the individual games more interesting and more understandable. It can't really be so complex and confusing when a Jerry Kramer can call his world "Camelot." And it isn't.

PRO FOOTBALL TODAY

Since the game of professional football arrived on the sports scene . . . 71 years ago . . . there have been many changes, both tactical and personnel-wise. During the infant years of the game, teams met when and wherever they could get together. Players often performed for several teams at the same time. The rules were those of the home team. Titles were often secured with the expediency of a mere press announcement, and, in general, the scene was a disorganized one.

Leagues came and went, and it wasn't until 1921, when the National Football League was formed, replacing the American Professional Football Association founded only a year before, that any semblance of order came about.

Franchises in the NFL at that time cost 50 dollars, and the league began play with 12 teams: Green Bay, the Canton Bulldogs, the Cleveland Indians, the Dayton Triangles, the Akron Professionals, the Massilon Tigers, the Rochester (N.Y.) Kodaks, the Rock Island Independents, the Decatur Staleys, the Chicago Cardinals, plus Muncie and Richmond, Indiana, whose team names were lost almost as quickly as their franchises.

That was the beginning, and the league set out on a note of optimism under the guiding hand of President Joe F. Carr, who remained in that role until his death in 1939. That initial optimism was to prove premature by some 25 or 30 years. Teams came and went almost as fast as the players. With the formation of the New Orleans Saints the number of franchises granted by the NFL alone reached 73, of which there are only 16 survivors. And, as has often been pointed out by the NFL's elder statesmen, there were few, if any, of those franchises now numbered among the missing who died a voluntary death.

Even entire leagues sprang up during the fledgling years of pro football. Probably the most disastrous attempt at a competitive league was the All-American Conference, which was formed just after World War II and collapsed four years later.

The AAC, however, did leave its mark on the NFL. The Cleveland Browns and the San Francisco Forty-Niners, two of its financially stable members, made the shift to the older league and have been eminently successful.

In 1959, that "other league," the American Football League, was formed, and while there were to be many rocky years ahead, a glance at the ownership roster was enough to assure oneself that it was here to stay. Lamar Hunt, K. S. "Bud" Adams, Ralph Wilson, Jr., and Baron Hilton were four of the original owners, and their financial statements alone assured the success of the AFL.

Lamar Hunt, who was to be one of the principal architects of the NFL-AFL merger some seven years later, was named the first President of the AFL, and war hero Joe Foss became its first Commissioner.

Multi-million dollar anti-trust suits, lawsuits over players who signed contracts with both leagues, and sparse crowds marked the early days of the AFL. Franchise shifting, reminiscent of the early days of the NFL, were also part of those rocky days through the early sixties, but as much as the older NFL wanted to see the AFL go away, it would not.

The battle for player talent reached a climactic peak in 1964 and '65. College stars were caught up in the dollar war, and while many were "shocked" by the offers and counter-offers, the youngsters made the most of a "players' market" that by the end of 1965 threatened to break both leagues.

The merger came with dramatic suddenness before the season of 1966. Pete Rozelle became the Commissioner of both leagues, Milt Woodard the President of the AFL and Art Modell the President of the NFL. A common player draft was formulated and a post-season meeting of league champions in 1966 was announced. Inter-league play and player trading was put off until 1970 because of conflicting television contracts and players' pension programs, but the big hurdle had been crossed.

Was the merger necessary? Absolutely. Both leagues were spiraling toward bankruptcy, and the nation's fans, the most important asset to pro football, were getting disgusted with big men acting like children. These same fans also wanted to see the two league champions meet, something they saw in January of 1967 when the Green Bay Packers defeated the Kansas City Chiefs, 35 to 10, before an estimated television audience of 70 million.

Peace, or at least an armed truce, had arrived once again for pro football, and the AFL, which merged with eight teams, expanded to ten in 1967 with the addition of Cincinnati, a franchise bought for over seven million dollars that, prior to the merger, would have been considered worthless.

While the economics of the game has changed the structure of professional football, the tactics and strategy and the men who perform on the field have also undergone tremendous changes from those early years. Today the game is played with a scientific approach that was undreamed of in the days of Nagurski and Grange. The offensive setups are a far cry from the few simple plays that were employed in the early years, while the defense in the past ten years has emerged to where it is a game unto itself, played and comprehended only by those who make that phase of the game their specialty.

In a word, "specialty" describes the game of pro football today. There are 22 positions on a football team, encompassing 16 different and highly specialized "jobs." They are, on offense, the center, the offensive guards, the offensive tackles, the tight end, the flanker, the split end, the halfback, the fullback, and the quarterback. On defense, there are the ends, the tackles, the outside linebackers, the middle linebackers, the corner backs, and the safeties — free and tight. These specialists operate basically from what I'm sure you've heard referred to as the standard pro offense and the standard pro defense.

Below is the on-field set for both, with the offense facing the defense.

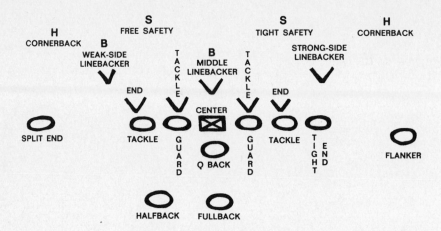

The following is a brief sketch of the positions that make up the pro football teams of today. I'll begin with the defense because, while I made my major marks as an offensive player, I firmly believe that defense is where championship teams are born.

Actually, it's a simple deduction. For a team to win, it has to get points, and prevent points. The defense is involved in both. They must stop the offense of the opposition and they must also turn the ball over to their highly publicized teammates frequently, and in the best field position possible. The defensive specialists are highly aware of this responsibility, and while you can find occasional defensive stars who might covet some of the attention lavished on their offensive hero teammates, they nevertheless approach their work with a great deal of pride.

I can recall a rather embarrassing happening for one Giants' offensive team of the early sixties that might point up just how seriously the defensive players take their jobs. It was during our division winning streak and we were playing the Cowboys on a hot September afternoon in the Dallas Cotton Bowl. We were midway through the second period and while our defensive team had not given up a point, our highly publicized offensive team, with the likes of Y. A. Tittle, Del Shofner, Rosie Brown, etc., had failed to make so much as a first down. It was one, two, three downs and kick . . . and out would go the defensive team again with hardly so much as a chance to catch their breath from the last encounter. Over and over it happened, we'd give up the ball, the defense would take the field, scratch and claw, and get it again for us.

Finally, it got to the point where we wouldn't look the defensive club in the eye as we passed each other at the change of the ball. They were hot, sweaty, and bloodied; and we had hardly even soiled our uniforms. It reached a climax when Sam Huff, the captain of the defense and our great middle linebacker, recovered a fumble, turning the ball over to us once again. As we took the long route to the scrimmage line to avoid the 22 glaring eyes of a by now thoroughly teed-off defensive team, Huff interrupted his return to the bench and planted himself right at the spot where we would have to huddle. As we grouped around, eyes downcast, Sam addressed us with some rather choice adjectives. Through the blood and sweat he allowed that, "By God, we've got it for you again. Now the least you can do is hold them for awhile."

I would imagine the tremendous pride generated by great defensive units can be attributed to the lack of the "key individual" situation that's found on offensive teams. There are players that are exceptions, but by and large, a defensive team is successful only as a team, whereas an offensive club can be built around one or two or several individual stars.

THE DEFENSE

Defensive Ends

In the basic four-three defense, the defensive end must have the size, generally in excess of 240, to meet pulling guards intent on trapping him while the ball carrier cuts inside the end and outside the tackle. He must also have great strength to overcome a double-team block by the offensive tight end and the offensive tackle. He must have speed and agility to go with this size, as he is first and foremost in the forward-pass rush. On the pass rush to the quarterback, he is generally met first by the offensive tackle, who seldom weighs in at less than 250 pounds. After clearing the tackle, he often must face a smaller but capable blocking halfback or fullback . . . all of this while keeping in mind that the average passer will generally release the ball some four or five seconds after the snap. He also needs this speed and agility in pursuit of plays that break to the outside. As we will see, the defense is designed to turn outside plays back into the pursuit and the defensive end is that pursuit.

Defensive Tackle

If there was ever any position I lacked all incentive to play, it has to be the defensive tackle.

This is the heart and soul of a defensive club. It's where, in modern terminology, you could say, "It all happens." The tackle lines up just inside of the defensive end in the "four-three" and he is faced with the quick, hard-hitting offensive guards, and flanked by the offensive center and tackles. In other words, he is vulnerable, to say the least. He needs exceptional strength to fight off blocks coming down by the tackle, or out by the center. On short yardage, when the offense attempts straight-ahead wedge blocking for the score, or first down, he alone is responsible for piling it up and back. This he does with sheer strength.

I was once asked what was the biggest difference between the professional game and the collegiate game. This was after I had played my first year, and after thinking for only a moment I said it was the tremendous noise that takes place all round you when you run inside, against the pros. At the college level, there are thuds and occasional pops of leather and headgears, but with the pros, those thuds take on volcanic proportions, often accompanied by dire threats on one's life, accented with the most basic adjectives.

This is the result of the defensive tackle at work, the strong boy of the defense, and a man respected by his teammates more than any other.

Outside Linebackers

I've often maintained that if there is indeed a mean personality required on a football field, it's at the linebacker's spot, and I don't think this peculiar breed of player has let me down.

Linebackers are like smallpox to receivers and running backs; they're to be avoided if at all possible. Linebackers work up close to the battle zone and they get hit from all sides. They generally are smaller than linemen, ranging from 215 pounds to 250 pounds. Their accent must be on speed, although they need the strength and the toughness to fill holes at the line of scrimmage and stop a running back in his tracks.

In recent years they have been called on with ever increasing frequency to take part in the pass rush, red-dogging the quarterback from outside, or looping inside the defensive end and rushing in through the heavy traffic. When they are not red-dogging, they must be equipped with enough speed to drop into areas of pass protection often 20 yards down the field.

In short, the requirements for the linebacker are speed to stay with the little man, size to handle the big man, and an intelligence to read offensive keys that will give him the jump on the coming play. There are a few great ones; it's a position that's hazardous in terms of injuries, and this special breed is hard to find.

Middle Linebacker

Without a top-flight middle linebacker, a defensive football team is less than great. It's that simple. The best defense in pro football is the four-three, and you can't play the four-three without a top MLB.

Middle linebackers, according to Giants' defensive coach Harland Svare, are born, not made. I suppose this observation was arrived at by Harland when once, several years ago, he was forced to move to the middle spot from the outside linebacker position because of an injury to Sam Huff. It was an exhibition game against the Forty-Niners in Salt Lake City, and to this day Harland, who was an outstanding outside linebacker, recalls how completely lost he was at the middle spot.

The middle linebacker, in the four-three, lines up between his defensive tackles about two yards off the line of scrimmage. His principal responsibility is the running game from end to end. He must fill all holes that are opened from tackle to tackle, and also be in position to nail ball carriers being turned back to the inside on sweeps.

He must have, if not great speed, a quickness that will get him into the line to meet the runners before they gain room to maneuver, and he must have strength to fight off blocks by the guards, tackles, and ends.

Most good MLB's seem almost intuitive when it comes to being where their offensive play is going, and while it often appears they are psychic, it generally means they are so well versed in what the offensive opponent will run on certain situations that they can anticipate the huddle call by the quarterback.

In the pass defense, the MLB, like the outside linebackers, must be able to range far back in the defense to take away certain passing areas, and also have the strength and quickness to red-dog the quarterback from any hole, tackle to tackle.

Defensive Corner Back

The most lonely spots on a football field are manned by the defensive corner backs. Their jobs are to cover the speedy outside receivers that operate as split ends and flankers. They are also responsible for turning to the inside end runs, and in this role they often must meet head on the offensive guards, who generally convoy the runner on end sweeps. While covering the receivers is difficult work, taking on 250-pound guards is the kind of work that can get you two to three weeks off with pay.

Defensive corner men vary a great deal in size . . . some are tall and slight, others short and stocky . . . but they have one thing in common; they are all quick and they are all fast. This is an absolute necessity, as the receivers they cover are the fastest men in the game.

Covering the receiver on a pass pattern from the corner is often a lonely and unrewarding proposition. Since the receiver knows exactly where *he* is going on each pass pattern, and the defender has only the slightest suspicion based on the game situation, it's logical to conclude that the receiver should win each and every encounter.

However, the corner back has several subtle things going for him. He knows that if his defensive teammates are in a red-dogging defense, he will not have to stay with the receiver as long as he would under ordinary circumstances. He can play the receiver closer because the quarterback will not have much time to throw the ball against the red-dog. When the red-dog is not on, the corner back covering a receiver knows that he can anticipate help from the linebackers, who now will be dropping back into pass zones, forcing the quarterback to throw over their heads to complete the pass. In this situation, he can play a little further off the receiver, and should, because while the quarterback must now thread the ball between linebackers for a completion, he also has more time in which to hold the ball before the release is necessary.

As you will see in the defensive chapter, there are other helps the "lonely one" has on defense, but as any corner man will tell you, against a top receiver, when the quarterback has time to throw the ball . . . accurately . . . their job is impossible.

Safeties

There are two roles to the safety position in professional football. One is the free safety, who plays on the side of the offensive split end; the other is the "tight safety," who plays on the side of the offensive tight end.

On some teams, these two positions are separate, with the free safety always assuming that position regardless of the offensive formation, and the tight safety doing likewise. For instance, the New York Giants and St. Louis Cardinals always play in that fashion, while the Green Bay Packers' safeties always remain on the same side, Willie Wood to the right and Tom Brown to the left. This requires the Green Bay safeties to know both the roles of the tight safety as well as that of the free safety.

If you will check the illustration of the standard pro offense on page 18, you will see that the tight safety is lined up just outside the offensive tight end. He plays anywhere from five to ten yards deep, and is basically man-to-man on the tight end if a pass play develops. The free safety has no tight end on his side in the standard pro defense, and his basic assignment is to take the offense halfback if he comes out of the backfield on a pass pattern or, if not, assist either the tight safety or the corner back on his side. This we will go into further in the chapter on defense.

Safety men need much the same physical equipment as the corner backs. They must have the speed to stay with receivers that range both deep and short, and they must have the size to meet a running back who has broken through the line and linebackers.

THE OFFENSE

The offensive units of professional teams, like the defensive teams, are highly specialized and yet similar as you go from team to team. While teams offer varied formations and attacks, they basically evolve from similar set-ups...the standard pro offense.

Center

The center's responsibility in offensive line play is not merely to make sure he gets the ball to the quarterback. He is in effect the quarterback of the offensive line. He is the one who calls the defensive line "set," to all offensive men on the line. He alerts his tackles and guards as to what type of blocking will be necessary to run the play that has been called in the huddle. For instance, an off-tackle play against an odd-man line will require considerably different blocking than against an even line, and since he is at the hub, he is best situated to evaluate what the exact defensive set is.

He must also have the size and quickness to handle the big defensive tackles, the men he is most often called upon to block. He also must have good lateral movement as he is frequently called upon to pull out of the line and block outside linebackers who are rushing the quarterback as red-dog men.

Guards

Maybe the most difficult job in pro football is handled by the offensive guards. By necessity, they must be big men, yet they must also have the speed that pulling and leading interference for an end run requires. They must be in absolute top condition, as they often lead interference around one end on one play, and come back on the next play and lead interference around the opposite end. When the play calls for them to block straight ahead or pass-block, their principal assignments will be on the biggest men on the field, the defensive tackles. Consequently, the offensive guards must be the most versatile blockers on the line.

Offensive Tackles

The tackle positions in pro football are manned by the biggest of the offensive personnel. Their principal assignments are the handling of the defensive end, on both running and passing plays. They play a vital role in the pass offense, as the strongest pass rush is usually applied from the defensive-end position. They, along with the guards, must not let their men penetrate to the quarterback's passing zone, and they must be agile enough to make sure the end doesn't go around them, either to the inside or the outside.

Tight End

The tight end must be part guard, part tackle, and part split end and flanker. He must be big enough to block alone on a linebacker or defensive end for the running play, and agile enough to move downfield into a pattern on a pass play. Because the offensive formations go both right and left, he must be able to block from both sides (which isn't the easiest thing to do).

The patterns the tight end runs are generally, but not always, of the shorter variety and he is often the man who is called on to go after the ball in a "group."

The turn-in over the middle to the tight end is a favorite of many teams on a third and sure pass situation. Here the tight end must be able to escape the mauling of the strong-side linebacker, who always lines up right over his head, and releases downfield. After clearing the linebacker, he must beat the man who is covering him man for man, the tight safety. He must command enough respect from the safety to drive him downfield, and then with a hooking maneuver, turn in and face the quarterback.

Whether he catches the ball or not, he is almost always going to get a pretty good shot in the back as the safety man recovers and drives back into him to break up the pass. You've probably heard the expression "He heard footsteps." Well, this is where it originated. It's tough for a receiver to turn his back to a defender and wait for the ball to arrive. He calculates mentally how much time he has before the defender will have recovered, and how long it takes the ball to arrive. It's amazing how often those time lapses coincide, and seldom does a receiver catch a pass of this nature without taking the resultant punishment.

Split End

For pure longevity, this would appear to be the position to play. A split end can go through an entire quarter of a ball game and hardly be noticed. His role is one of threat almost as much as action.

He lines up on either side opposite the flanker and usually ten or more yards wide of the offensive tackle. The man he works on primarily in the passing game is the corner back.

He's almost always one of the fastest men on the field, since he must range deep for the long bomb, and the faster he does the more difficult he is to cover, and the safer it is for his quarterback. Height is an asset, but there have been many fine split ends who were, and are, in the six-foot bracket.

On the split-end side, most of the pass patterns are of the individual nature, meaning it's man on man, the split end versus the corner back. However, a top split end will often find that he will be double-teamed, by either the linebacker on his side or the free safety. This requires a thorough knowledge of defense and the open areas where the quarterback can deliver the ball.

And, like all receivers, the split end must be able to impart information voluntarily, or when asked by the quarterback. In my 12 years under two quarterbacks, Charlie Conerly and Y. A. Tittle, I was often asked in the huddle what I could do against a certain defender. I tried always to have a play ready for any situation, and many times when you see a particularly beautiful pass pattern work to perfection, it is the result of an alert receiver passing on information the quarterback ordinarily would never have been aware of.

Halfbacks

The halfbacks in pro football today have become much like their running partners, the fullbacks. So much so that many teams now simply refer to the two as set backs and let it go at that.

However, on many teams the assignments and requirements differ a great deal. Most teams use their halfbacks for the wider plays, the sweeps and pitchouts. Physically, they may resemble the fullback; however, most are faster and more agile since this is what outside running requires. Still, they are bigger now than ever before, and are getting bigger. They must have speed and power, power to burst through tackles at the line of scrimmage, and speed to outrun the pursuer after they are once in the open field.

They are used a great deal in successful pass offenses, and they work principally against linebackers and the free safeties. Size and strength has become a very important prerequisite for the halfback, as the linebackers have grown in size over the years. The halfback deals with this "ornery" breed more than any other offensive player. He must avoid them on leaving the backfield on a pass pattern. He must block them on pass protection, when they red-dog, and he must be able to take their punishing tackles when he is the ball carrier.

There are many halfbacks who are also adept at throwing the forward pass. It isn't a definite requirement, but any coach with imagination will tell you it is a most welcome asset to have a halfback who can start out on an end run, pull the defense up, and fire a pass downfield. Many a ball game has been broken up by this maneuver.

Fullbacks

The fullback, as we mentioned, has a lot of duties in common with the halfback. He must be able to run pass patterns, although that is not his primary duty. He must be able to handle the red-dogging linebackers, when protecting for the passer, and most important, he must be able to get the extra yard when needed. Often the outcome of a ball game has hinged on whether or not a team's fullback can scratch out a first down on a third- or fourth-and-one yardage situation. This is where the men are separated from the boys, as often the fullback is forced to make his own hole if the yardage is to be made. Like the halfback, speed is a great help, and quickness is absolutely necessary.

Quarterback

A professional football team can do a lot of things without a top-notch quarterback. One of the things they can't do with any consistency is win. A quarterback is the heart and soul of the offense. He is the one who sets the play into motion, first in the huddle, and then at the line of scrimmage.

In my 12 years with the Giants, I was fortunate to play with two great ones, Charlie Conerly and Y. A. Tittle. On the surface, these two men are decidedly different personalities. Y. A. was a gregarious, bubbly individual, whose enthusiasm and love for the game were reflected in his every move. A bad play on the field, on his part or a teammate's, might cause Y. A. to snatch off his helmet and slam it to the turf, while all the time exposing an absolutely bald and gleaming head.

In the huddle or on the sidelines, Y. A. was always thinking and working a game. He was at your side in the locker room, before the game and at half time, probing for information, digging out that one defensive flaw you might be able to offer that, mixed with other ingredients, might spell the difference. Y. A. knew the game and he knew it well. The game he knew was his . . . hit them when they were not expecting it . . . and this he did better than any other quarterback. He'd probe it with the run, but his specialty was the pass. He had a sidearm delivery that in his prime was the most accurate arm in the game. In total, Y. A. was excitement and a great quarterback.

Charlie Conerly was the antithesis of Tittle. Charlie gave the impression of almost boredom, both on the field and off, and sometimes it wasn't just an impression. He was relaxed at all times, and the tougher the game, the calmer he would become. He was a great athlete in that he could do just about anything with his body, from golf to horseshoes to football. It was all natural.

Off the field, until Charley became a nationally known figure, few people would ever recognize him as a great quarterback; as a matter of fact, you could point him out, and they wouldn't believe you. He was prematurely gray in his great years, the fifties, and absolutely gray in his last few years. And those last few years were his greatest.

In the huddle in a tight game — where Y. A. gained his mates' confidence with optimistic enthusiasm on each play — Charley accomplished the same thing without effort. A tense do-or-don't situation might receive the following in huddle treatment from these two great pros.

Where the outcome of a game might hang on a single play, Y. A. would enter the huddle, and you could feel the excitement. "Okay, this is it now . . . I need time to get it off... Now come on chief, pick up that dog... he's been getting to me... if we blow this one we've blown the whole damn thing... okay now, dammit, keep 'em out of here... flanker right, 1 X right, L zig in..." It was excitement and it commanded attention.

Charley, however, commanded the same respect and got the same effort in the following manner. In a slight Southern accent, his command would be, "Okay now, I'll need a little more time on this . . . flanker right . . . L zig in... and I guess we'd better run a 1 X on the right. . . ." It came slow and deliberate and there was no doubt in your mind it would work.

I've described the completely opposite personalities of these two great quarterbacks to point up that football's most important position, quarterback, can be manned by a variety of individuals. Yet there are certain physical requirements, and one common denominator, that I'll get to in just a moment.

First the physical requirements, and first and foremost, today's professional quarterback must have a great arm. He must be able to throw long and short, be able to fire it on a string between linebackers, or lay it up between defenders far downfield. Timing of the release is probably his most important asset. This is not something that you teach. It is an instinct that seems to be inborn.

The quarterback doesn't have to be a strong physical specimen; better put, he must be "tough." During the season he might go through many games in which he will get nary a bump. Then again, he might take an absolutely inhuman beating on any given Sunday. A mental toughness is also involved, as the quarterback — unlike any other players who hit and get hit during the action — takes his punishment in a very vulnerable position, generally the moment after the pass delivery. Often he must stand in the pass pocket until he can release the ball, while all hell breaks loose around him. Amid this confusion he must be aware of how his pass blocking is holding up, how long before he can release the pass to an uncovered receiver downfield, and then make an instant evaluation as to whether he'll be able to get "it" off.

All these thoughts... knowing and disregarding the fact that buried under half a ton of defensive linemen, he'll probably never see whether the pass he released was caught, dropped, or intercepted.

The quarterback in today's game is also the man who walks in the glare of praise or criticism. He takes the brunt of the abuse (along with the coach) when things go wrong, and he receives most of the praise when things go right. Both are generally far out of proportion to the fact, but they are side elements today's quarterbacks must live with.

His discipline must be such that he will give up extra hours devoted to preparation. Those hours may be spent on the field, timing out a special pass with a receiver; or they may be hours spent with his coach looking at game films of the opposition, searching for the slightest weakness that can be exploited and magnified on game day.

Now the one thing all top quarterbacks have in common is that they are leaders. I've already pointed out that Charley Conerly and Y. A. Tittle were distinctly different personalities, yet they commanded respect and extra effort on the field. Bobby Layne, a funloving guy with the quick quip, was that way. While he'd laugh and live it up with the best off the field, on the field it was all business and 100 percent, and anyone who lagged more than likely would hear about it. Johnny Unitas has it, not only in respect for his accomplishments, but by example, for no player works harder than John in preparing for a game. He is often the last to leave the practice field, and the last to leave the skull and film sessions.

I suppose all the great ones over the years have had it. I can visit with Sid Luckman today and know he did. I've played All-Star games with Norm Van Brocklin. He had it in spades. The Waterfields, the Van Brocklins, the Conerlys, the Laynes, the Tittles — they all have what Don Meredith, Bart Starr, Fran Tarkenton, Daryle Lamonica, Joe Namath, and several others have today. They were winners; they didn't know any other game. And in pro football, there is no other game.

DEFENSIVE FOOTBALL

Defensive football, as I have said, to my way of thinking is the basis for winning football. The offense, to be sure, is the glamour of the game, but you don't win unless the defense gets the ball, number one, and number two, stops the opposition from scoring.

The offensive and defensive units of a professional football team are two distinct and almost unrelated teams. They practice, hold their meetings and chalk talks separate and apart, and take a great deal of pride in "their" unit's accomplishment on the field.

This individuality of respective units has created a competitive spirit that in most cases is an asset to a football team. No matter what the Monday morning newspapers report, the players themselves know who is really responsible for a victory. And if, as an offensive player, you've been part of a sputtering attack that was "bailed" out time and time again by the defensive unit, they're not about to let you forget it during the next week's practice session.

Similarly, an outstanding effort by the offensive unit in overcoming defensive mistakes or deficiencies will provide a sharp point to the "needle" applied delicately to the defense throughout the coming week.

Defensive football, up until the nineteen-fifties, lagged far behind the offense. Players were aligned in a multiplicity of defenses without any real thought to the science of applying a special defense to a specific offense. The many defenses which preceded today's standard professional defense are important only in how they contributed to the four-three, the present primary defensive setup.

Cleveland's Paul Brown had a great deal of success with a five-three alignment in his winning days of the fifties.

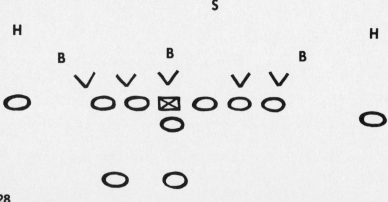

Bill Willis, the Browns' middle guard, was the key for Paul Brown in this defense. Willis was not big by today's standards, but he was perhaps the quickest defensive lineman I've ever seen. The five-man front could work against the run only, because Willis, moving like a cat, could beat the centers and two guards through the gaps of the 0 and 1 hole.

Teaming with the middle linebacker, who hit the opposite gap from Willis, the Browns were in effect using a six-man line while showing a five-man line prior to the snap of the ball.

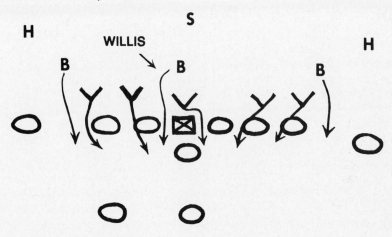

Teams attacked the Browns with a running game, feeling they could beat the five-man defense that was shown, while actually they were meeting a six-man front.

The weakness of the Browns' five-three was in the secondary. With only three men in the deep positions (two halfbacks and a safety), there were open zones for the deep hook passes that could not be covered.

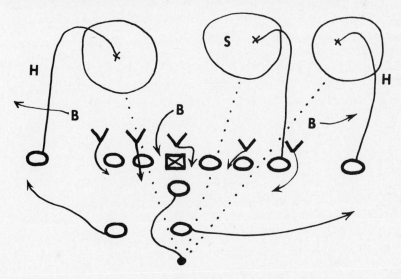

While the Browns were operating, and winning title after title, with their five-three, the New York Giants under Steve Owen (with a strong influence by Tom Landry, then a player-coach) were operating probably the best defensive unit in football. The Giants used a six-man front, and a four-man deep secondary, the latter a development of Earl "Greasy" Neale of the Philadelphia Eagles.

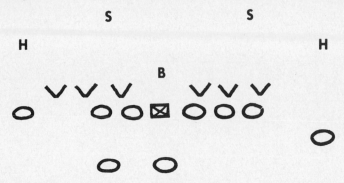

As was the case with the Cleveland Browns, teams began to look for ways to beat the Giants' six. And they found them again in the pass game. With six linemen up front, and no linebackers, the Giants could not cover halfbacks and fullbacks coming out of the offensive backfield. Nor could the four-man deep secondary cover the deep hook patterns of receivers, like Cleveland's Mac Speedie and Dante Lavelli, without linebacker help underneath.

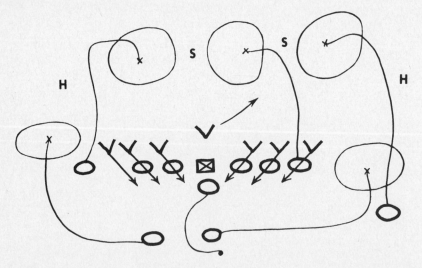

The deficiencies in the Giants' six-four led directly to the four-three. Tom Landry, playing safety at that time, and assisting as coach, decided with tackles like Arnie Weinmeister and Moose Krause, he didn't need a six-man line at all times. He was getting beat in the flats and the deep hook zones by the pass, and he came up with a solution that was simple and very lasting.

On a sure pass situation, Landry would take his defensive ends (at that time Jim Duncan and Ray Poole) and drop them off the line, where they would play like linebackers.

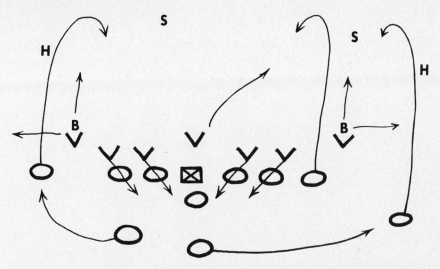

Landry was to find out that, because of his size and the strength of his guards and tackles, he could also use this defense quite effectively against the run. His next step was to replace his defensive ends on the six-man line with linebackers, who while smaller in size were more agile at doing the job at hand — covering the pass receivers coming out of the backfield and assisting the four-man secondary. This was the arrival of the four-three.

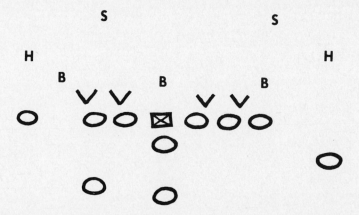

I know there are many who will say, "Come on now, Frank, I watch pro football all the time and I know teams don't always play the four-three," which, I might add, on the surface is a very valid observation. However, the following might serve to clear up some of the mystery that surrounds the defensive game, while at the same time point out that what you're seeing isn't always what you're seeing.

First of all, let's understand that the running game of football has two basic concepts. On the offense, you must open holes; and on the defense, you must close them. Now from there, let's look at the assignments of the men in the four-three.

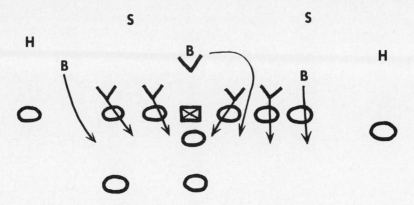

As you can see, each defensive man has a hole or gap for which he is responsible. The above is an inside four-three, used mainly when a defensive team is anticipating the offense to run between the tackles. Now let's look at a different defense that appears the same before the snap of the ball.

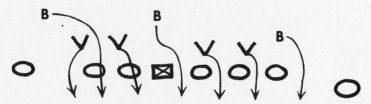

The above is an outside four-three. As you can see, the same gaps are covered, only by different bodies.

Now let's take a look at the principal odd-men lines that have developed over the last few years. They're called by many teams Frisco defenses, because, quite simply enough, it was the San Francisco Forty-Niners who first used them in the mid-fifties. Below is the first of the Friscos.

This particular defense was developed as teams started to beat the four-three with power end runs to the flanker side. As you can see, it is an overshift of linemen to the strong side (the flanker side) and an undershift of the linebackers to the weak side (the split end side). When first used, this defense was very effective at stopping the power sweep to the flanker side, a sweep used by nearly every team in football.

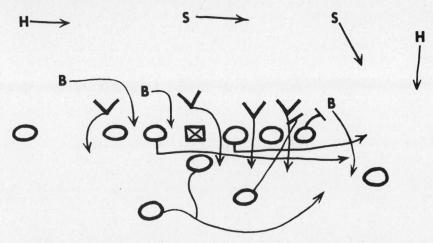

However, while the strong side Friscos had obvious strength against the strong side sweep, it had an obvious weakness to the weak side, and the power slant by the fullback.

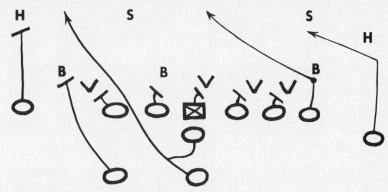

As more and more teams began to run back to the weak side against the strong-side Frisco, defensive coaches came up with the weakside Frisco.

The above defenses — the inside four-three, the outside four-three, and the Frisco weak and the Frisco strong — represent the most frequently used defenses in football today. They are called and used by the defensive quarterback when, according to his study of the opponent's offensive frequencies, he determines what offensive play he must anticipate.

Now let's go back to my premise that most all defenses do the same thing, even though they appear to be different. We've already seen that in the four-three inside and the four-three outside, all defensive gaps are filled, if not by the same man, at least with a body. Now let's examine the Frisco odds — first the Frisco strong.

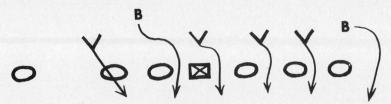

Again the holes or gaps are filled with bodies. And while the bodies belong to different people, all holes are nevertheless filled. The same is true with the defense below, the Frisco weak.

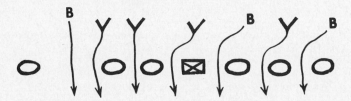

What I've tried to prove is that no matter what the face of the defense (and many teams scramble the alignment), when the ball is snapped, each man has an assignment, an area to fill, and he must move to that area. And, with all things considered, the personnel makeup of the four-three is the best possible way the defense can handle all situations.

THE DEFENSIVE SECONDARY

The defense against the forward pass, like the defense against the run, has evolved into a very scientific game within a game. As in every phase of football, there are variations, but by and large the secondary alignment of all pro teams is the four-man deep. This consists of two corner backs, two safety men, and the three linebackers.

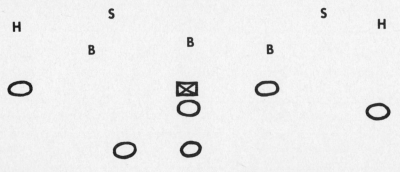

Each man has an individual assignment. Below is an offensive receiver setup against the basic four-three pass coverage. The receivers are numbered 1 through 5, with the corresponding man-to-man coverage indicated on the defense.

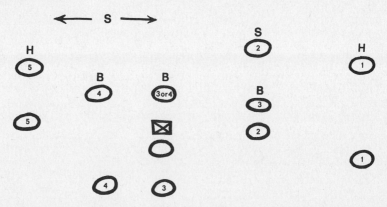

This diagram illustrates how the term "free safety" was coined. Notice that the safety on the split end side has no definite assignment. He is "free" to help the corner back on his side, or help the tight safety, or the opposite corner man deep.

On a red-dogging situation, which involves the weak-side linebacker, rushing the passer, the free safety is no longer free. Now his assignment is the set back on his side, and he must play him close because the linebacker in the pass rush cannot offer help underneath.

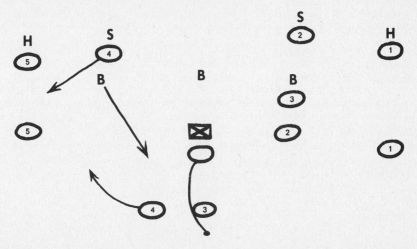

The above also illustrates how you, as a fan (or offensive quarterback), can read (anticipate) a red-dog by the weak-side linebacker, the most frequent red-dog in pro football. Notice how the free safety has now moved up closer to the line of scrimmage, in contrast to his position in the standard man-to-man defense, where he is free to roam and help. This is one key quarterbacks look for in reading a red-dog, and so can you.

In recent years, the safety red-dog has become a very popular defense. It is used by teams that must gamble because they lack strong secondary coverage and cannot afford to allow a quarterback time to throw, or by teams with exceptionally strong man-to-man coverage who can afford the risk because of exceptional coverage downfield. Below is the safety dog blitz.

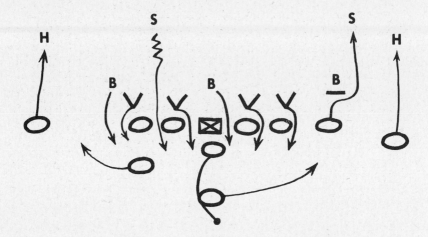

As you can see, the safety dog blitz, employing the free safety and linebackers in the pass rush, can give the defensive team a sometimes overpowering pass rush. If a quarterback has sent his backs into a pass pattern, there simply are not enough offensive blockers to handle the rush.

The disadvantages and hazards are almost as obvious. Number one, if a quarterback has anticipated the safety dog, he will have kept his backs in to pick up the rush.

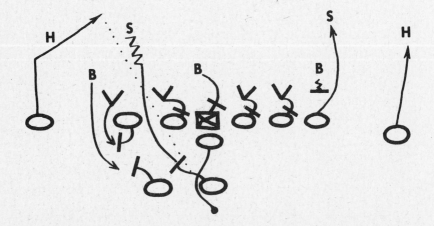

The above allows a quarterback time to throw the ball and puts his receivers into the desired position of operating one on one against the corner backs and tight safety, who are covering without benefit of help from the free safety or the linebackers.

The safety red-dog has "bit" a lot of quarterbacks, but the top signal callers in the past couple of years have made the gamble more and more hazardous.

Becoming frequently more popular in defensive football today is the "change of face." Simply put, this means the use of multiple fronts (the four-three, the Frisco odds) and multiple secondary coverages.

We've already analyzed the primary frontal alignment of teams and explained that while they may appear different and might offer momentary confusion to a quarterback and his blocking line, they boil down to basically the same thing.

This is not true, however, in the secondary. Again, the most frequently used defense is the pure four-three-four, with man-to-man coverage.

Now let's suppose the split left end on a team is an exceptional receiver that will be difficult for the corner man to cover, alone, in the man to man. The defensive quarterback wants to help his corner man so he calls "four-three key weak". . . (or a similar designation). This alerts the secondary and linebackers to the following coverage.

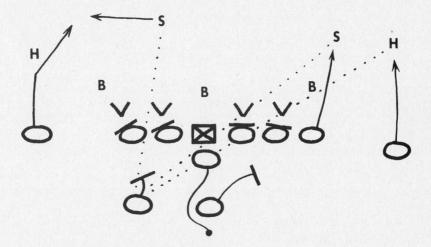

You see now that the troublesome receiver is double-covered by the free safety and the corner back; the tight safety is man to man with the tight end, and the left corner back is man to man with the flanker.

The "key" has been the blocking halfback, and all the defensive secondary get their key at the snap of the ball from him. If he blocks, all will know automatically what their pass coverage will be . . . (the double coverage on the split end, the single coverage on the tight end and flanker).

If he should not block, but comes out on a pass pattern, the key might be called off and the coverage revert to man to man, or the double coverage might still remain, with the offensive halfback now covered by the weakside linebacker, as in the following.

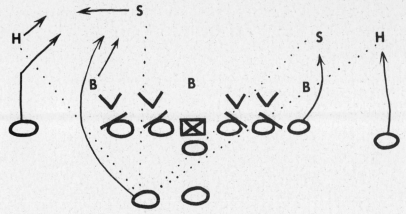

The "key" coverage can also be used to double-cover an annoying tight end or flanker, with the following coverage indicated by a defensive huddle call such as "four-three key strong" (the "strong" referring to the tight end or flanker).

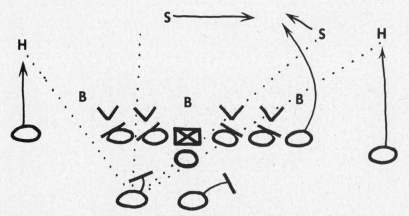

Another way in which a defense can get added protection against a dangerous receiver is by the use of the zone defense. There are several such defenses, but the following are the most frequently used.

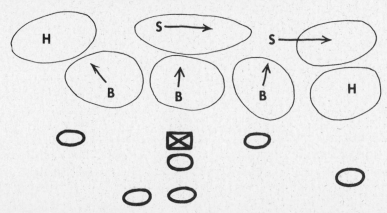

The preceding is the purest of the zones, and the defense means just what it says. Each man in the secondary and the linebacking corps has a zone for which he is responsible. The corner backs on the flanker side now covers a short zone area, the tight safety the deep area behind the corner back, the free safety the deep middle, and the weak-side corner back — while remaining in a man-to-man situation — can now play a little looser, because he knows he has linebacker help underneath and help to the inside from the free safety.

One disadvantage to the above is that when a team wishes to use the zone to the wide side of the field, the tight safety often has to show the quarterback before the snap of the ball that he is going to be in the pure zone. In other words, to get to his deep position at the snap of the ball, he must line up wider than usual.

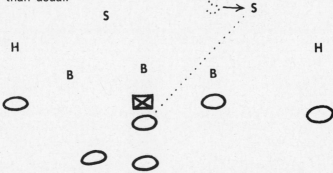

Since there are certain pass patterns that work exceptionally well against the pure zone, the above tipoff will allow an alert quarterback to recognize the pure zone and change the play to a more favorable one.

As a result of this weakness another zone defense has come into being. It is called the safety zone defense, and accomplishes the same thing as the pure zone without any pre-snap tipoff.

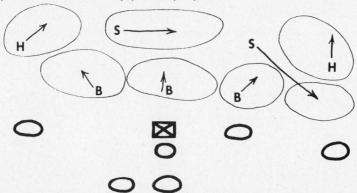

The preceding, of course, has many more subtleties than I have gone into. One of the most important of these subtleties deals not with theory but attitude. That basic attitude is one of confidence, in oneself, the defense, and one's teammates. As you can see, each man has an assignment built on the assignment of a teammate, and the strength of the overall defense is only as strong as the weakest link.

OFFENSIVE FOOTBALL

The offensive game in professional football, unlike the defense, differs a great deal from team to team. This is understandable, as the offense on nearly all teams is built for and around key individuals, whereas there are few, if any, solid defensive teams built around two or three key players.

Still, the face of the offense for all practical purposes is the same on all teams, and has been referred to as the standard pro offense.

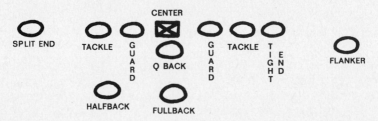

This offensive formation, like the standard pro defense, came into being in the early fifties. Like the standard pro defense, it didn't just arrive on the scene accidentally, but evolved from other formations and as a result of necessity.

Let's first look at the most basic of offensive formations.

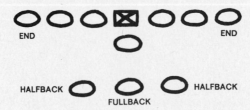

The above can be called the pure T-formation. I doubt seriously if many modern pro football fans can ever recall seeing this formation used in a game. However, years ago this was *the* formation of football.

The demise of this formation came about with the development of the forward pass, and passers such as Sammy Baugh, Sid Luckman, and Bob Waterfield. Inhibited by this formation in that their receivers could not get off the line of scrimmage (and when they did they were still in a confined area), coaches first started experimenting with the splitting of one receiver.

This innovation to the offensive game can probably be traced back to the Los Angeles Rams of the late forties and early fifties and their coaches, Clark Shaughnessy and Joe Stydahar, although even at that time other coaches were already experimenting with freeing their receivers from the confinement of the "in-tight" positioning.

The Rams, however, had the equipment necessary to go several steps further than their competition. They had talented receivers aplenty in Tom Fears, Glenn Davis, Bob Boyd, Elroy Hirsch, and Vitamin Smith. They also had three enormous running backs in Tank Younger, Deacon Dan Towler, and Dick Hoerner, who were able to blast open holes on their own.

It was probably the ability of these three big men to gain yardage on their own that brought about the further changes in the pro football offense. The big blocking ends were no longer a necessity to the Rams' running game, so why not give your passer further tools with which to work on the defense? Bob Boyd, a big 9.5-second sprinter who had been wasting away on defense was put out as one split end. Tom Fears was split to the other side and Elroy Hirsch operated in what was to become known as the slot.

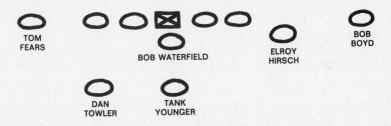

TOM FEARS   BOB WATERFIELD   ELROY HIRSCH   BOB BOYD

DAN TOWLER   TANK YOUNGER

Now all of a sudden defensive teams were seeing an entirely different offensive picture. The defensive backs were being forced to cover three speedy, tricky receivers in the open field, and they were just not up to it. In 1950 these three men caught 168 passes, and the Rams won the Western Division titles for three years running, 1949-1951.

If there's one thing coaches are not ashamed of, it's taking from another coach. With the Rams' success came duplication throughout the entire league. The Detroit Lions put Doak Walker out as flanker and Cloice Box as the split end, and they took over dominance of the Western Conference, with Bobby Layne at the passing helm. The Browns put Dante Lavelli one way and Mac Speedie the other and they took charge of the East, and Otto Graham began to rewrite the record books.

Most teams still operate 75 percent of their offense from that standard pro offense developed first by the Rams. In the ensuing chapters, which will deal with each individual team, we'll attempt to get a line on the offensive pattern of each teams and the whys thereof.

Right now, let's consider the overall goal of an offensive team, and that is to maintain and move the football. There are only a few on-the-field situations in football. These same situations apply to both the defense and the offense. They are: first down and ten yards to go; second down and short yardage (one to four yards); second down and long yardage (five yards plus); third down and short yardage (one to three yards); third down and long yardage (four yards plus). There are other special situations, such as fourth and one, which come into consideration according to a specific situation at a given time in a game.

With each of the above situations, a game of chess occurs in both the offensive and defensive huddles on each play. Teams develop "frequencies" of what they like to do in any given situation, whether it's on the offense or the defense. This happens because quite simply they like to do (in each given situation) what they can do best.

A hypothetical situation might be the following. Cleveland is playing Dallas; the game is scoreless midway through the second quarter, and it's third and seven for the Cleveland offense against the Dallas defense.

Both teams know the following from intensive study of the opposition's previous game's films, and the personality of the respective teams: the Dallas defensive quarterback knows that of all the plays at hand, Cleveland's quarterback Frank Ryan will probably go with what he considers his best play for this situation; he knows that in the past Ryan has "liked" to throw the ball on third and long, and now he must decide which of his receivers Ryan will most likely go to; flanker back Gary Collins has been Ryan's third-and-long man 38 percent of the time, and Collins' best pattern is a short down-and-in — 21 percent of the time Ryan has gone to halfback Ernie Green on a circle pass over the middle — 12 percent of the time Ryan has given the ball to Leroy Kelly on a draw play up the middle, and so on; the best percentage defense Dallas can offer is to stop Collins first, Green second, and Kelly third. Therefore, and the decision must be made in only a matter of seconds, the Dallas defensive quarterback might call a "four-three outside, strong-side key." This would give Dallas double coverage on Collins, with the corner man and the free safety, and offer protection against Ernie Green coming out of the backfield on the pass.

Meanwhile, in the offensive huddle, Ryan also has many considerations. He knows from his study of game films that the Dallas defense is not prone to red-dog on third and long. Their frequency in previous games is to stay with the four-three while attempting to double-cover the opposition's top receiver. Ryan also knows that the Dallas quarterback knows that Ryan likes the Collins pass in the situation at hand. Ryan must therefore assume that Dallas will be in a four-three, no red-dog, and double coverage on Collins.

Now the decision. Is the Collins pass strong enough to go with, when almost surely it's anticipated? Or should he use Ernie Green coming out of the backfield, or should he go back to the other side and use receiver Paul Warfield, who'll more than likely, as a result of the double coverage on Collins, be covered alone by the corner back? He might turn to Collins and ask, "How about it, Gary, the down-and-in?" Collins, a gifted and experienced receiver, won't lie to him, and will either answer with a quick affirmative, or a hesitant, "It'll be tough." Ryan thinks, "I know they won't, but what if I put Kelly in the pattern and they dog? Boy, what a time to go for the big one to Collins on a zig-out [a fake down-and-in with a break to the outside]." He might remember Dallas' corner back Cornell Green, intercepting one of his passes in a similar situation a year ago.

He makes the call . . . "What the hell, they haven't stopped Collins all day. Why leave it?" "Formation right," he says (sending Collins to the flanker and splitting Warfield). "Y. Down-and-in" (Collins' call for the down-and-in). "A flare" (Green's call for a flare to the opposite side). "On three" (the number on which the ball will be snapped). Leaving the huddle, he might quickly tell Green to be "looking," the last comment expressing his own apprehensions that Dallas won't do what they're supposed to do.

The Dallas defensive quarterback has also had many variables to think of. "Ryan is smart as hell. He knows we'll probably use the four-three key. What if he throws the bomb to Warfield and catches us in that single coverage? If he runs that draw to Kelly up the middle against that outside four-three, it's liable to go all the way." He might even think, "Why doesn't coach Landry send in the right defense? Look at him there, drinking out of the water bucket when I sure as hell could use some help."

And so it goes, the offense working against the defense with what they do best, and the defense setting their alignment to meet the expected and hoping to stop the unexpected. It happens on each and every play, and the cumulative results over a 2-hour and 40-minute period spell victory or defeat.

The most recent departure from the standard pro offense has been the ever-increasing use of the flanker formations. The most widely used of these is the double flanker.

The reason for the use of the double flanker is to force a defense to play man for man; in other words, get rid of the zone and free-safety situation. As we've pointed out, the free safety can be a bothersome nuisance to a quarterback when he is left free to help one or more defenders, as he is defending against the standard pro offense.

However, as you can see in the preceding diagram, against the double flanker he is no longer free; his man, the halfback, in the standard pro offense is now moved to the outside, near the line of scrimmage, and is an immediate threat on a pass. Therefore, he must now work man-to-man against his man, and cannot roam and help.

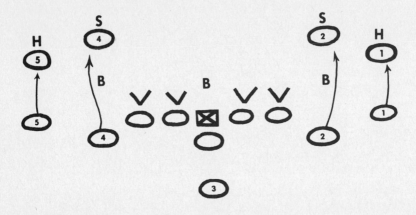

There are a multiple number of flanker formations now being used in pro football. Some are used to get a specific receiver covered by a specific defender whose ability is not too highly regarded, but basically they are all designed to force the defense to play straight man-to-man.

THE NATIONAL FOOTBALL LEAGUE   1968

EASTERN CONFERENCE

Capitol Division
Dallas Cowboys
New York Giants
Philadelphia Eagles
Washington Redskins

Century Division
Cleveland Browns
New Orleans Saints
Pittsburgh Steelers
St. Louis Cardinals

WESTERN CONFERENCE

Central Division
Chicago Bears
Detroit Lions
Green Bay Packers
Minnesota Vikings

Coastal Division
Atlanta Falcons
Baltimore Colts
Los Angeles Rams
San Francisco Forty-Niners

DALLAS COWBOYS

When I listen to coach Tom Landry talk football today, it's almost as if I were going back to 1952 and '53 when, as a corner back, I played with safety man Tom Landry.

Tom, as he did then, takes the mystique out of the game, reducing every phase to the simplest form of execution, while at the same time burdening the opposition as much as possible.

In leading his Cowboys to the top of the NFL's Eastern Division, Landry has built a team that carries out this philosophy. His multiple offense is designed to burden the opposition's defense, and his defense is one of the most solid and consistent in football.

Tom has picked his personnel with great care over the years, building up a team that has for the past two years taken the NFL Eastern Division title. He is a firm believer in the four-three defense, and, as we have pointed out, he was one of its principal architects. The Cowboys led the league or have been near the top of the NFL's offense for several years, and that accomplishment, as well as their overall success, has been largely due to an opportunistic defense that kept taking the ball while holding down the point production by the opposition.

The key man, if there is one in the Dallas defense, is tackle Bob Lilly. Lilly is the man you must concentrate on if you are going to throw or run against Dallas. When you watch the Cowboys, you'll notice that Lilly, when lined up on the weak side, appears to be almost offside. Lilly can play this close because of his amazing quickness. Playing in this position, Lilly removes

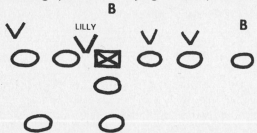

the opposition's ability to run the power sweep because the guard playing opposite him cannot pull to the strong side. Lilly's move from this position is a slashing, penetrating one that also complicates the guard's job on the pass block. Many times Lilly will be in the quarterback's face before he ever has a chance to get the ball away.

The rest of the Dallas front four are almost the equal of Lilly. Jethro Pugh plays the other tackle, and Willie Townes and big George Andrie hold down the end positions. The linebackers are Lee Roy Jordan at the middle spot, and Dave Edwards and Chuck Howley at the corners. Both Howley and Edwards are good red-doggers. Although the Cowboys are not known as a major red-dogging team, when they do shoot linebackers, it is usually the weak-side linebacker and comes on second and long yardage.

In the secondary, the Cowboys seldom use other than man-to-man coverage. All four deep backs are drilled in keys, and with the start of each offensive play, they know from whom and where they can expect help.

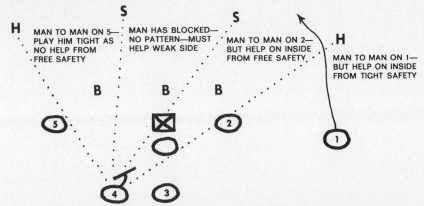

S   S

H MAN TO MAN ON 5—   MAN HAS BLOCKED—   **H**
PLAY HIM TIGHT AS   NO PATTERN—MUST   MAN TO MAN ON 2—
NO HELP FROM   HELP WEAK SIDE   BUT HELP ON INSIDE
FREE SAFETY   FROM FREE SAFETY.   MAN TO MAN ON 1—
        BUT HELP ON INSIDE
        FROM TIGHT SAFETY

In the above, the left corner back has keyed the offensive halfback, who has stayed in to block. He now knows that he will receive help from the safety man on his side, because the left safety, also keying the offensive halfback, knows that the right safety is free to help him to his inside (because his man, the offensive halfback, is now blocking).

It sounds somewhat complicated, and it is even a little more involved than stated. Yet the Dallas secondary is the best in the business at reading their keys, and while all this happens in the fraction of a second after the ball is snapped, they seldom make a mistake.

On offense, the Cowboys are almost impossible to defend against. They show nearly every formation in the book, with receivers switching from right to left. They have tremendous speed at the flanks. Bob Hayes, at split end, heads this parade as the world's fastest human.

Dan Reeves and Don Perkins, the running backs, are also fine receivers, as are flankers Lance Rentzel and Pete Gent, and tight end Pettis Norman.

Don Meredith is a first-rate passer and signal caller, and more important, he is a leader that demands, and gets, extra effort.

One thing the Cowboys have going for them is that Bob Hayes is such a touchdown threat, he generally must be double-covered. As a result, Norman at the tight end and Rentzel at the flanker seldom see more than one-man coverage. With this single coverage on the strong side, the Cowboys often use the following pass to their tight end on third and long.

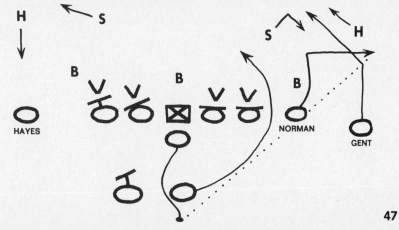

Still, the instant scoring threat for the Cowboys is Bob Hayes. If he ever gets into the open, it's all over. He runs several patterns well, even when he is double-covered. One, of course, is when he just takes off and defies anyone to stay with him, and Meredith lets it go with all he's got. To my knowledge, he's never been able to overthrow Hayes.

Another pattern Hayes likes is a simple deep square-in, with Meredith hitting him when and wherever he happens to be.

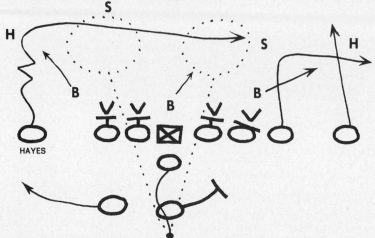

Still another pass the Cowboys like to throw to Hayes is the hitch screen. On this pass, Hayes starts downfield, and any defensive cornerman in his right mind will start back with him. Hayes pulls up after about three yards, steps back towards the line of scrimmage, and Meredith hits him. Meanwhile, the tackle has pulled flat down the line of scrimmage to take the defensive halfback, who is now recovering. This play is designed to spring Hayes into the open field, and is often used on third-and-desperate situations, such as third and 15 to 25.

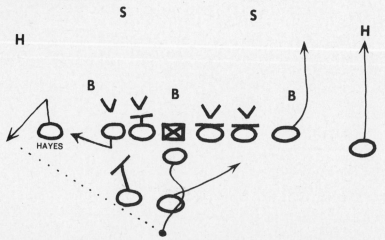

In summation, the Cowboys are solid throughout. They have electrifying speed and are drilled and coached as well as any team in football.

DALLAS COWBOYS   1968 Veterans Roster

NO.	NAME	POS.	HT.	WT.	AGE	YRS. IN NFL	COLLEGE
66	Andrie, George	DE	6-7	250	28	7	Marquette
46	Baynham, Craig	RB	6-1	206	24	2	Georgia Tech
68	Boeke, Jim	T	6-5	260	29	9	Heidelberg
37	Clark, Phil	DB	6-2	210	22	2	Northwestern
53	Connelly, Mike	C	6-3	248	32	9	Utah State
45	Daniels, Dick	DB	5-9	180	23	3	Pacific (Ore.)
83	Deters, Harold	K	6-0	203	24	2	N. Carolina State
26	Dial, Buddy*	FL	6-1	185	31	9	Rice
62	Donohue, Leon	G	6-4	245	29	7	San Jose State
79	East, Ron	DT	6-4	242	25	2	Montana State
52	Edwards, Dave	LB	6-1	228	28	6	Auburn
27	Gaechter, Mike	DB	6-0	190	28	7	Oregon
32	Garrison, Walt	RB	6-0	205	24	3	Oklahoma State
35	Gent, Pete	FL	6-4	205	26	5	Michigan State
34	Green, Cornell	DB	6-3	208	28	7	Utah State
22	Hayes, Bob	E	5-11	185	25	4	Florida A&M
54	Howley, Chuck	LB	6-2	225	32	10	West Virginia
23	Johnson, Mike	DB	5-11	184	24	3	Kansas
55	Jordan, Lee Roy	LB	6-1	225	27	6	Alabama
74	Lilly, Bob	DT	6-5	260	29	8	TCU
72	Liscio, Tony	T	6-5	255	28	5	Tulsa
51	Manders, Dave*	C	6-2	250	27	4	Michigan State
17	Meredith, Don	QB	6-3	205	30	9	SMU
14	Morton, Craig	QB	6-4	216	25	4	California
73	Neely, Ralph	T	6-6	265	24	4	Oklahoma
76	Niland, John	G	6-3	245	24	3	Iowa
84	Norman, Pettis	TE	6-3	225	29	7	J. C. Smith
43	Perkins, Don	RB	5-10	200	30	8	New Mexico
75	Pugh, Jethro	DT	6-6	260	24	4	Elizabeth City State
30	Reeves, Dan	RB	6-1	200	24	4	South Carolina
20	Renfro, Mel	DB	6-0	190	26	5	Oregon
19	Rentzel, Lance	FL-E	6-2	200	24	4	Oklahoma
13	Rhome, Jerry	QB	6-0	185	26	4	Tulsa
67	Schmitz, Bob**	LB	6-1	235	29	7	Montana State
25	Shy, Les	RB	6-1	200	24	3	Long Beach State
77	Stephens, Larry	DE	6-3	250	29	9	Texas
31	Stokes, Sims	E	6-1	197	24	2	N. Arizona
71	Townes, Willie	DE	6-4	260	25	3	Tulsa
11	Villanueva, Danny	K	5-11	200	30	9	New Mexico State
57	Walker, Malcolm	C-T	6-4	249	25	3	Rice
65	Wilbur, John	G	6-3	240	25	3	Stanford
85	Wright, Rayfield	TE	6-7	243	22	2	Fort Valley State

*Dial and Manders missed entire '67 season because of injuries
**Last active in NFL with Minnesota in 1966

DALLAS COWBOYS   1968 Top Rookies

NAME	POS.	HT.	WT.	AGE	COLLEGE	HOW ACQUIRED*
Douglas, John	LB	6-2	212	23	Missouri	D-4
Harmon, Ed	LB	6-4	240	22	Louisville	D-3
Homan, Dennis	E	6-1	181	22	Alabama	D-1

NAME	POS.	HT.	WT.	AGE	COLLEGE	HOW ACQUIRED*
Lewis, D. D.	L B	6-2	210	23	Stanford	D-6
McDaniels, David	E	6-4	200	23	Missouri Valley	D-2
Nye, Blaine	T	6-4	255	22	Houston	D-17

*D — Draft (Number indicates draft round)
FA — Free Agent

(The lists of top rookies in each of the chapters on the individual teams obviously do not name all of the first-year men who will be in camp. The few I have mentioned are merely the most likely prospects to survive the training period and find a place on the regular roster. This list was compiled through evaluating the rookies' college career, the needs of the respective team, and through conversation with coaches and officials of the various clubs.

Have I missed a potential super-star? I can only tell you that in last year's Guidebook under "Green Bay Packers Rookies," I failed to list Travis Williams as a likely candidate to make the team. So, my belated apologies to Travis and my apologies in advance to those players whom I'm sure I've missed this year.

The complete team rosters obviously will have undergone some change as a result of trades, retirements, and other events, between our publishing date and the beginning of the season. However, it's highly improbable that these changes will have any major effect on the majority of the clubs.)

DALLAS COWBOYS 1968 Schedule

Sept. 15 — Detroit	1:30		Nov. 3 — at New Orleans	1:00
Sept. 22 — Cleveland	1:30		Nov. 10 — New York	3.00
Sept. 29 — at Philadelphia	1:15		Nov. 17 — at Washington	1:15
Oct. 6 — at St. Louis	1:00		Nov. 24 — at Chicago	1:00
Oct. 13 — Philadelphia	1:30		Nov. 28 — Washington	5:00
Oct. 20 — at Minnesota	1:30		Dec. 8 — Pittsburgh	1:00
Oct. 28 — Green Bay	8:30		Dec. 15 — at New York	1:30

NEW YORK GIANTS

The New York Giants are presenting a team in 1968 that is on the way up.

The most outstanding change is at the all-important quarterback spot, where Fran Tarkenton, a seasoned, if sometimes unconventional, runner-passer is now holding forth. Head coach Allie Sherman, as he did when he won divisional titles in 1961-62-63 with Y. A. Tittle, has molded his offense to Tarkenton's specific talents. Contrary to what many observers think, Tarkenton does not run helter-skelter all over the football field on a whim. He is a very thoughtful young man, with multiple talents few quarterbacks have ever possessed.

His arm is a strong one—he can throw short or long with the best of them—and he has the plus of being a gifted runner. The label of scrambler has been tacked on Tarkenton because of his running ability. Actually, I'm sure that over the years there would have been many more quarterbacks with the same label had they been given the same ability. In other words, when the pass protection breaks down, and not until then, does Tarkenton become a running passer.

This talent also gives Fran more time to throw the ball than most quarterbacks, because a defensive pass rusher must be more cautious in his rush or he'll grab a handful of air.

Aside from Tarkenton's famed running exploits, and they are something to behold, this young man from Georgia has a career passing record of over 53 percent completions, 142 of his passes going for touchdowns.

Tarkenton is aided a great deal by a top pass-receiving corps that has a lot of speed and savvy. Aaron Thomas, who can operate from either the tight end or the flanker, has potential that is still untapped. He has great speed, and from the tight-end position runs the following pass pattern better than any other tight end in the league.

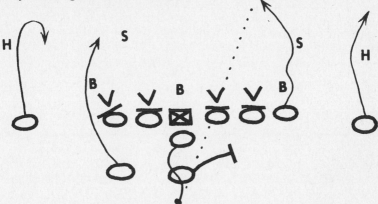

At split end is Homer Jones, who is big, strong, and speedy. Jones, who has been clocked in 9.3 for the hundred, can do a lot of things, but what he does best is the straight fly down the field, in a sprint with the defender. He is also an exceptionally strong runner once he gets his hands on the ball; therefore, the Giants like the following play to Homer.

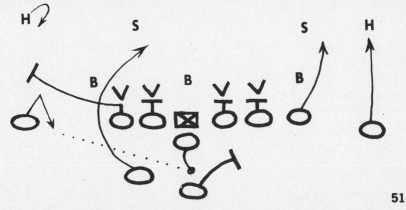

The Giants' running game came up with a big shot in the arm last year with the incredible improvement of third-year man Ernie Koy. Koy gained over 700 yards last year, at a nearly five-yard average, and he gained most of it as a marked man after Tucker Frederickson injured a knee.

The Giants still have hopes for Frederickson, who for the second consecutive year has undergone knee surgery. If Tuck can't make it back (and no one has ever worked harder in the attempt), the Giants can go with either Bill Triplett or youngster Randy Minniear, who came up from semi-pro ball and showed well at the conclusion of last season.

The Giants overall possess an extremely talented offensive team that last year was a consistently high scoring unit. At the center spot is Greg Larson, who quarterbacks the line; at the guards are Pete Case and Bookie Bolin, both quick and hard-hitting.

Look for Tarkenton to use receiver Aaron Thomas a great deal on clutch situations, and Homer Jones when he wants to hit from far out. Koy will be the man called on for the short yardage, and then for just pure enjoyment, watch Fran Tarkenton when he's forced to run out of the pocket.

Defensively, the Giants have been looking for the man who can give them the consistent pass rush. You can't win in pro football unless you make the opposition respect your pass rush, and Allie Sherman knows this. Big Bob Lurtsema helped in that area last year, but Allie knows he still needs to put more pressure on enemy passers.

Now, under the tutelage of defensive coach Harland Svare, the Giants are back to the fundamental four-three. And while they still make mistakes, they do so with less frequency and without the earth-shaking results of last year.

The linebacking department will be vastly improved this year with the acquisition of Tommy Crutcher from Green Bay. He comes with top credentials, even though playing behind the best in the business at Green Bay he didn't see much action. Bill Swain has completely recovered from knee worries and Mike Ciccolella, along with veteran Vince Costello, are more than adequate in the middle.

In the secondary, the Giants are counting on great things from second-year man Scott Eaton. Last year as a rookie he showed tremendous potential, not only in man-to-man coverage, but by displaying the little touch of viciousness that is needed for the corner spot.

Spider Lockhart should also improve after a year of indoctrination as a free safety, while the verdict is still out on Willie Williams at corner and Freeman White at the tight safety.

In summation, the Giants are building an offense around Tarkenton and talented receivers who can score enough to compensate for a defense that, while strong in certain areas, is decidedly weak in others.

NEW YORK GIANTS   1968 Veterans Roster

NO.	NAME	POS.	HT.	WT.	AGE	YRS. IN NFL	COLLEGE
79	Anderson, Bruce	DE	6-4	250	24	3	Willamette College
73	Anderson, Roger	DT	6-5	265	27	5	Virginia Union
54	Avery, Ken	LB	6-1	220	23	2	Southern Mississippi
63	Bolin, Bookie	G	6-2	250	28	7	Mississippi
85	Brown, Barry	TE	6-3	235	25	3	Florida
65	Case, Pete	G	6-3	250	27	7	Georgia
48	Childs, Clarence	DB	6-0	180	30	5	Florida A&M
58	Ciccolella, Mike	LB	6-1	235	24	3	Dayton
72	Colvin, Jim	DT	6-2	250	30	9	Houston
70	Condren, Glen	DE	6-2	250	26	4	Oklahoma
57	Costello, Vince	LB	6-0	230	36	12	Ohio
89	Crespino, Bob	E	6-4	225	30	8	Mississippi
56	Crutcher, Tom	LB	6-3	230	26	5	TCU
76	Davis, Don	DT	6-6	280	23	3	Los Angeles State
77	Davis, Rosey	DE	6-4	260	26	3	Tennessee A&I
62	Dess, Darrell	G	6-0	245	33	11	N. Carolina State
20	Eaton, Scott	DB	6-3	195	23	2	Oregon State
24	Frederickson, Tucker	FB	6-2	230	25	4	Auburn
3	Gogolak, Pete	K	6-1	185	26	5	Cornell
64	Gross, Andy	G	6-0	235	22	2	Auburn
61	Harper, Charlie	T	6-2	250	23	3	Oklahoma
26	Harris, Wendell	DB	5-11	185	28	7	LSU
56	Hinton, Chuck	C	6-2	235	25	2	Mississippi
30	Jacobs, Allen	FB	6-0	215	26	4	Utah
45	Jones, Homer	E	6-2	215	27	5	Texas Southern
75	Katcavage, Jim	DE	6-3	240	33	13	Dayton
18	Kennedy, Tom	QB	6-1	200	29	3	Los Angeles State
23	Key, Ernie	HB	6-3	230	26	4	Texas
53	Larson, Greg	C	6-3	250	29	8	Minnesota
43	Lockhart, Carl	DB	6-2	175	25	4	North Texas State
71	Lurtsema, Bob	DE	6-6	250	24	2	Western Michigan
27	Minniear, Randy	HB	6-1	210	24	2	Purdue
74	Moran, Jim	DT	6-5	275	26	5	Idaho
11	Morrall, Earl	QB	6-2	206	34	13	Michigan
40	Morrison, Joe	HB	6-1	212	31	10	Cincinnati
84	Murdock, Les	K	6-3	245	24	2	Florida State
22	Post, Bob	DB	6-2	195	24	2	Kings Point
55	Smith, Jeff	LB	6-0	237	23	3	Southern California
83	Staten, Randy	DE	6-1	245	24	2	Minnesota
52	Swain, Bill	LB	6-2	230	27	6	Oregon
10	Tarkenton, Fran	QB	6-0	190	28	8	Georgia
88	Thomas, Aaron	E	6-3	210	30	8	Oregon State
38	Triplett, Bill	HB	6-2	210	27	6	Miami (Ohio)
25	Vargo, Larry	LB	6-3	225	30	8	Detroit
66	Van Horn, Douglas	G	6-2	245	23	2	Ohio State
51	Weisacosky, Ed	LB	6-1	225	24	2	Miami University
81	White, Freeman	DB	6-5	225	23	3	Nebraska
41	Williams, Willie	DB	6-1	190	27	4	Grambling
78	Wright, Steve	T	6-6	252	26	5	Alabama
69	Young, Willie	T	6-0	265	23	3	Grambling

NEW YORK GIANTS 1968 Rookie Roster

NAME	POS.	HT.	WT.	AGE	COLLEGE	HOW ACQUIRED*
Buzin, Richard	T	6-4	250	23	Penn State	D-2
Davis, Henry	L B-DE	6-3	235	23	Grambling	D-11
Duhon, Bob	R B-DB	6-0	190	22	Tulane	D-3
Holifield, Jim	D B	6-3	195	22	Jackson State	D-12
Koontz, Joe	E	6-1	192	22	San Francisco State	D-9
Parker, Ken	D B	6-2	185	22	Fordham	D-16
Thompson, Lou	G	6-2	240	22	Alabama	D-4

*D — Draft (Number indicates draft round)
FA — Free Agent

NEW YORK GIANTS 1968 Schedule

Sept. 15 — at Pittsburgh	1:30	Nov. 3 — Baltimore	1:30
Sept. 22 — at Philadelphia	1:15	Nov. 10 — at Dallas	3:00
Sept. 29 — Washington	1:30	Nov. 17 — Philadelphia	1:30
Oct. 6 — New Orleans	1:30	Nov. 24 — at Los Angeles	1:00
Oct. 13 — at Atlanta	1:30	Dec. 1 — at Cleveland	1:30
Oct. 20 — San Francisco	1:30	Dec. 8 — St. Louis	1:30
Oct. 27 — at Washington	1:30	Dec. 15 — Dallas	1:30

PHILADELPHIA EAGLES

Head coach Joe Kuharich has a basic philosophy that calls for an offense balanced between the pass and the run; on defense he is dedicated to playing a game that will keep the opposition guessing.

The Eagles live up to this philosophy on the field. They do the unexpected on defense, such as red-dogging on any and all situations. They red-dog the safety and have been known to red-dog both safeties, a hazardous but very upsetting proposition for enemy quarterbacks.

The Eagles also show multiple secondary defenses that feature straight man-to-man (always on red-dog situations) and zone defenses. Nate Ramsey and Joe Scarpati are exceptional performers from their safety positions, with Scarpati the key man in the Eagles' safety red-dog.

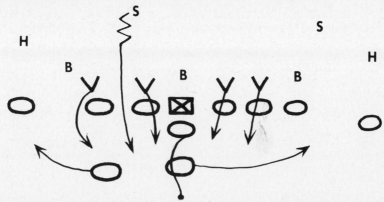

At the cornerbacks are youngsters Jim Nettles and Al Nelson, both of whom have great speed, and while prone to an occasional mistake, they make up for it with the ability to recover quickly.

At the middle linebacker position is Dave Lloyd, a highly underrated middle linebacker in my estimation. He is exceptionally quick, a good reader of plays, and a constant threat on the red-dog combination with outside linebacker Harold Wells.

While on the surface it may at times appear helter-skelter, it is in fact a sound defensive unit, with the strength of the whole predicated on individual performances. Of the front four, the key man against both the run and the pass is tackle Floyd Peters, a big veteran who also gives stability to youngsters Don Hultz and Mel Tom at the ends.

On offense, quarterback Norm Snead runs the whole show, and while occasionally erratic, he is at times brilliant. Mike Ditka, who went through a tough injury year last season, is expected to be the Eagles' big third-down man this year, and no one can run the turn-in pass over the middle better than Mike.

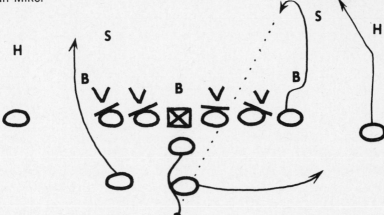

Gary Ballman, acquired before the '67 season from the Steelers, makes the Eagles' passing attack that much stronger. Ballman is a big, strong competitor who can also fight for the ball and run away from defenders when he gets it. His favorite pattern is the deep down-and-in, and the Eagles like it for the score on first and ten, and for the first down on third and long.

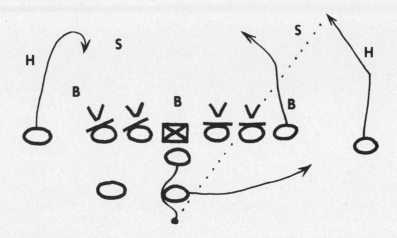

Ron Goodwin and Gary Ballman are the speedsters in the Eagles' passing attack. Both can range far down field, and Snead has the arm to reach them at any distance.

The Eagles' running game, now with Timmy Brown gone, may not be the most exciting thing in the world, but starters Israel Lang and Tom Woodeshick make up in strength and size what they lack in niftiness. Both are 230-pounders, and are also topnotch blockers for quarterback Snead. They primarily run inside, and if you want a thrill, watch tackle Bob Brown opening up holes on the right side.

PHILADELPHIA EAGLES   1968 Veterans Roster

NO.	NAME	POS.	HT.	WT.	AGE*	YRS. IN NFL	COLLEGE
38	Baker, Sam	K	6-2	218	35	14	Oregon State
85	Ballman, Gary	SE	6-1	205	28	7	Michigan State
64	Beisler, Randy	DE	6-5	255	23	3	Indiana
19	Berry, Dan	RB	6-1	214	24	2	California
76	Brown, Bob	OT	6-4	285	26	5	Nebraska
55	Brown, Fred	LB	6-5	237	25	3	Miami (Fla.)
4	Dial, Benjy	QB	6-1	185	25	2	Eastern New Mexico State
98	Ditka, Mike	TE	6-3	225	28	8	Pittsburgh
31	Emelianchik, Pete	SE	6-2	213	24	2	Richmond
81	Goodwin, Ron	FL	5-11	180	27	6	Baylor
78	Graham, Dave	OT	6-3	250	29	6	Virginia
28	Gray, Jim	DB	6-0	182	26	2	Toledo

NO.	NAME	POS.	HT.	WT.	AGE*	YRS. IN NFL	COLLEGE
71	Hart, Dick	OG	6-2	251	25	2	None
18	Hawkins, Ben	FL	6-0	180	24	3	Arizona State
30	Haymond, Alvin	DB	6-0	194	26	5	Southern U.
86	Hill, Fred.	SE	6-2	215	25	4	Southern California
10	Hill, King	QB	6-3	216	31	11	Rice
79	Howell, Lane	OT	6-5	272	27	6	Grambling
63	Hoyem, Lynn	C	6-4	253	29	6	Long Beach State
7	Huarte, John	QB	6-0	190	25	1	Notre Dame
13	Hughes, Chuck	FL	5-11	170	25	2	Texas (El Paso)
83	Hultz, Don	DE	6-3	242	27	6	Southern Mississippi
23	Jones, Harry	RB	6-2	205	23	2	Arkansas
51	Kelley, Ike	LB	5-11	222	24	3	Ohio State
84	Kelly, Jim	TE	6-2	219	26	4	Notre Dame
29	Lang, Izzy	RB	6-1	232	26	5	Tennessee State
87	Lince, Dave	DT	6-7	259	24	3	North Dakota
52	Lloyd, Dave	LB	6-3	248	31	10	Georgia
42	Martin, Aaron	DB	6-0	190	26	5	N. Carolina College
45	Medved, Ron	DB	6-1	195	24	3	Washington
75	Meyers, John	DT	6-6	276	28	6	Washington
74	Molden, Frank	DT	6-5	273	26	2	Jackson State
89	Morgan, Mike	LB	6-4	242	26	5	LSU
26	Nelson, Al	DB	5-11	186	24	4	Cincinnati
9	Nettles, Jim	DB	5-10	177	26	4	Wisconsin
72	Peters, Floyd	DT	6-4	255	32	10	San Francisco State
88	Pettigrew, Gary	DE	6-4	255	23	3	Stanford
24	Ramsey, Nate	DB	6-1	200	27	6	Indiana
50	Recher, Dave	C	6-1	241	25	4	Iowa
17	Reed, Taft	DB	6-2	197	26	2	Jackson State
21	Scarpati, Joe	DB	5-10	185	25	5	N. Carolina State
70	Skaggs, Jim	OG	6-3	252	28	6	Washington
16	Snead, Norman	QB	6-4	215	29	8	Wake Forest
62	Stetz, Bill	OG	6-2	248	24	2	Boston College
58	Tom, Mel	DE	6-4	249	27	2	San Jose State
61	Vasys, Arunas	LB	6-2	233	25	3	Notre Dame
53	Wells, Harold	LB	6-2	224	29	4	Purdue
41	Wilson, Harry	RB	5-11	205	23	2	Nebraska
82	Wink, Dean	DT	6-4	246	23	2	Yankton College
37	Woodeshick, Tom	RB	6-0	225	26	6	West Virginia
66	Wright, Gordon	OG	6-3	245	24	2	Delaware State

*Age as of Sept. 1, 1968

PHILADELPHIA EAGLES   1968 Top Rookies

NAME	POS.	HT.	WT.	AGE	COLLEGE	HOW ACQUIRED*
Dirks, Mike	OG	6-2	250	21	Wyoming	D-5
Lavan, Al	DB	6-1	194	21	Colorado State	D-8
Pinder, Cyril	RB	6-2	222	22	Illinois	D-2
Przybycki, Joe	G	6-2	244	21	Michigan State	D-7
Rossovich, Tim	DE	6-4	245	22	Southern California	D-1
Young, Adrian	LB	6-1	225	22	Southern California	D-2

*D — Draft (Number indicates draft round)
FA — Free Agent

PHILADELPHIA EAGLES   1968 Schedule

Sept. 15 – at Green Bay	1:00	Nov. 3 – St. Louis	1:15
Sept. 22 – New York	1:15	Nov. 10 – Washington	1:15
Sept. 29 – Dallas	1:15	Nov. 17 – at New York	1:30
Oct. 6 – at Washington	1:30	Nov. 24 – at Cleveland	1:30
Oct. 13 – at Dallas	1:30	Nov. 28 – at Detroit	12:15
Oct. 20 – Chicago	1:15	Dec. 8 – New Orleans	1:15
Oct. 27 – at Pittsburgh	1:30	Dec. 15 – Minnesota	1:15

WASHINGTON REDSKINS

Otto Graham, in his second year as head man of the Redskins, has molded a team very much to his liking. It is a team like the old Cleveland Browns, which Graham guided to titles in the early fifties, a quick-hitting, high-scoring team that also plays a solid, rugged, defensive game.

The big man on the attack for the 'Skins is quarterback Sonny Jurgensen, who had his finest season last year under Graham. Jurgensen, like the Graham of old, is a great passer. He has a tremendously strong arm for the deep passes and can shorten up to thread the needle between linebackers.

His receivers don't hurt matters either. Split end Charley Taylor, tight end Jerry Smith, and Bobby Mitchell are as good a combination as there is in football. Among them, they caught 197 passes last year, Taylor leading the league, Smith ranking second, and Mitchell fourth. Taylor is the man most feared of this threesome, and the following is one of his favorite routes.

58

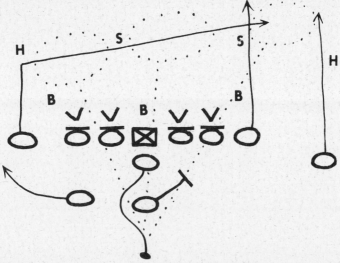

On the above, Jurgensen waits until he finds Taylor in the open and then connects. Taylor's many pluses include great speed and running ability. Consequently, the 'Skins like to get the ball to him in as many situations as possible. Like Bob Hayes of Dallas, he runs a good hitch screen, and Jurgensen will call the play on third and extremely long yardage when the defense is looking for a long pass rather than the short. He is also one of the best square-out men in the league on third-down situations.

What complicates matters for a team attempting to defense the Redskins is that it's almost impossible to double-cover Taylor, because then you're faced with Bobby Mitchell on the other side.

Mitchell has yet to slow up, and he's been around for a long time. He currently is the fourth most productive active pass catcher in the league. His best patterns are similar to Taylor's in that he likes the hitch (two steps and then catch it) and the square-outs. Mitchell is also a dangerous deep man, on the fly straight down the field. On this pass Mitchell, in combination with the tight end, bananas his route just enough to give Jurgensen a passing angle.

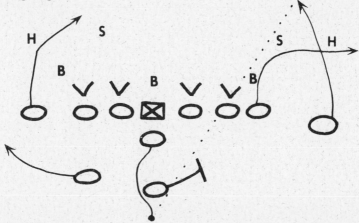

Mitchell and Taylor are men to watch on reverses, and any time they have the ball, they can go all the way.

The Redskins don't kid around; they are a passing team and they don't care who knows it. Consequently, they use many draw plays and fake draws to set up the pass game.

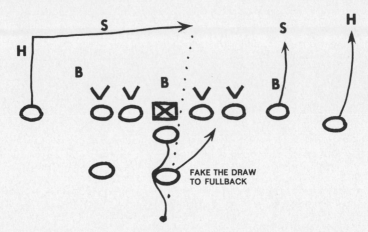

FAKE THE DRAW
TO FULLBACK

The Redskins' running game isn't the strongest in the league, and part of the reason could be that it doesn't get much exercise during the season. Jurgensen set a league record last year in passing, which can mean only one thing: the 'Skins simply don't run the ball very often. And A. D. Whitfield led that department last year for the Redskins, with a mere 384 yards. Consequently, the Redskins went heavy in the draft for running help, picking Bob Brunet of Louisiana Poly, Brian Magnuson of Montana, and Willie Turner of Jackson State.

The Redskins' defensive unit will be hurt throughout the year with the retirement of middle linebacker Sam Huff. He was their leader as well as an outstanding performer. Chris Hanburger, an exceptional linebacker on the outside, may work into this spot, but it will be a difficult transition.

The Redskins like to red-dog on second-and-long-yardage situations and third and long. One has to suspect that the 'Skins use the red-dog like the following to protect a secondary that, while adequate, has not been together as a unit consistently enough to be effective.

The 'Skins defensive front four is solidly anchored by defensive ends Ron Snidow and Karl Kammerer, and defensive tackles Joe Rutgens and Walter Barnes. They are experienced and would probably be rated higher in football circles had they the help of top-flight linebacking.

In summation, the Redskins have a rugged, not overly imaginative defense that gets the job done. When the 'Skins offensive team is on the field, the key word is pass.

Jurgensen, a master at cutting up a defense, is a pleasure to watch. The men he throws to are some of the best who've ever played the game, and when you watch one of them, Charley Taylor, you may be looking at the man who some day will be called the best.

NO.	NAME	POS.	HT.	WT.	AGE	YRS. IN NFL	COLLEGE
50	Adams, Willie	DE	6-2	235	24	3	New Mexico State
5	Alford, Bruce	K	6-0	190	23	2	TCU
20	Allen, Gerry	RB	6-1	200	26	3	Omaha
35	Baldwin, Bob	RB	6-0	220	25	2	Clemson
61	Bandy, Don	G	6-3	250	22	2	Tulsa
77	Barnes, Walter	DT	6-3	250	24	3	Nebraska
63	Breding, Ed	LB	6-4	235	24	2	Texas A&M
86	Briggs, Bill	DE	6-4	250	24	3	Iowa
42	Burson, Jim	DB	6-0	185	27	6	Auburn
48	Burrell, John	E	6-3	195	27	7	Rice
60	Carroll, Jim	LB	6-1	230	25	4	Notre Dame
57	Crossan, Dave	C	6-3	245	28	4	Maryland
37	Fischer, Pat	DB	5-9	170	28	8	Nebraska
3	Gogolak, Charlie	K	5-10	165	23	3	Princeton
55	Hanburger, Chris	LB	6-2	218	26	4	North Carolina
46	Harris, Rickie	DB	5-10	182	24	4	Arizona
56	Hauss, Len	C	6-2	235	27	4	Georgia
53	Jackson, Steve	LB	6-1	225	25	3	Arlington State
22	Jackson, Trenton	FL	6-0	180	24	2	Illinois
29	Jarvis, Roger	DB	6-2	205	24	1	Clemson
64	Johnson, Mitch	T	6-4	250	24	4	UCLA
9	Jurgensen, Sonny	QB	6-0	203	34	12	Duke
66	Kammerer, Carl	DE	6-3	243	31	8	U. of Pacific
75	Kelly, John	T	6-3	250	24	3	Florida A&M
24	Larson, Pete	RB	6-1	200	23	2	Cornell
32	McDonald, Ray	RB	6-4	240	23	2	Idaho
—	McKeever, M.	TE	6-0	236	29	8	Southern California
49	Mitchell, Bob	FL	6-0	196	33	11	Illinois
71	Musgrove, Spain	DT	6-4	275	22	2	Utah State
11	Ninowski, Jim	QB	6-1	207	32	11	Michigan State
23	Owens, Brig	DB	5-11	190	25	3	Cincinnati
76	Prestel, Jim	DT	6-5	265	31	9	Idaho
65	Promuto, Vince	G	6-1	245	30	9	Holy Cross
88	Richter, Pat	E	6-5	230	27	6	Wisconsin
72	Rutgens, Joe	DT	6-2	255	29	8	Illinois
62	Schoenke, Ray	G	6-4	250	27	5	SMU
47	Shorter, Jim	DB	5-11	185	29	7	Detroit
28	Smith, Dick	DB	6-0	205	24	2	Northwestern
87	Smith, Jerry	E	6-2	208	25	4	Arizona State
78	Snidow, Ron	DE	6-3	250	26	6	Oregon
74	Snowden, Jim	T	6-3	255	25	4	Notre Dame
42	Taylor, Charley	E	6-3	210	27	5	Arizona State
17	Theofiledes, Harry	QB	5-10	180	24	1	Waynesburg
44	Thurlow, Steve	RB	6-3	222	26	5	Stanford
43	Walters, Tom	DB	6-2	195	26	5	Mississippi Southern
25	Whitfield, A. D.	RB	5-10	200	26	4	North Texas State
67	Williams, Sid	LB	6-2	235	26	5	Southern U.
52	Wingate, Heath	C	6-2	240	23	2	Bowling Green

WASHINGTON REDSKINS 1968 Top Rookies

NAME	POS.	HT.	WT.	AGE	COLLEGE	HOW ACQUIRED*
Banks, Willie	G	6-2	237	22	Alcorn A&M	D-6
Beban, Gary	Q B	6-1	195	21	UCLA	Trade
Crane, Dennis	D T	6-6	260	22	Southern California	D-4
Roussel, Tom	L B	6-3	235	23	Southern Mississippi	D-2
Smith, Jim	D B	6-3	195	21	Oregon	D-1
Stipech, John	L B	6-3	238	23	Utah	D-12, '66
Talbott, Danny	Q B	6-0	185	23	North Carolina	FA

*D—Draft (Number indicates draft round)
FA—Free Agent

WASHINGTON REDSKINS 1968 Schedule

Sept. 15 — at Chicago	1:00		Nov. 3 — at Minnesota	1:30
Sept. 22 — at New Orleans	1:30		Nov. 10 — at Philadelphia	1:15
Sept. 29 — at New York	1:30		Nov. 17 — Dallas	1:15
Oct. 6 — Philadelphia	1:30		Nov. 24 — Green Bay	1:15
Oct. 13 — Pittsburgh	1:30		Nov. 28 — at Dallas	5:00
Oct. 20 — at St. Louis	1:00		Dec. 8 — Cleveland	1:15
Oct. 27 — New York	1:30		Dec. 15 — Detroit	1:15

CLEVELAND BROWNS

Two years ago, Cleveland Browns' coach Blanton Collier stated, "You can't lose a player like Jimmy Brown and not be hurt. However, I feel our ground game will continue to be one of the best in the league."

Collier's statement wasn't merely whistling in the dark, as Leroy Kelly and Ernie Green picked up the load and made their coach look like a prophet. That next season (1966), the one-two punch of the Browns' running game were the most effective combination in the NFL, and last year they even improved on the previous year with Kelly becoming the league's best, while gaining 1,205 yards.

Collier brings to the coaching game a philosophy that "you can do almost anything you want to, if you are willing to work hard enough to accomplish it and you don't care who gets the credit."

The Browns' offense is one of the best-rounded in football. Led by quarterback Frank Ryan, they play a ball-control game that collects points while minimizing the opposition's opportunity to score.

Kelly and Green owe much of their success to a great blocking offensive line, in particular the two guards, John Wooten and Gene Hickerson. At tackle are Dick Schafrath and Monte Clark, and at center is Fred Hoaglin, all exceptional blockers for both the run and pass.

One of the Browns' key offensive plays is their power sweep, with Leroy Kelly carrying the ball. On this play, which the Browns run so effectively,

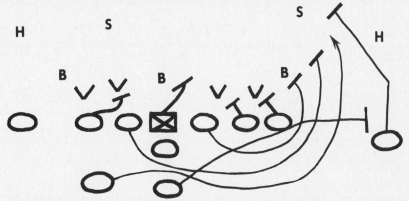

the key blocks are by Wooten, the left guard, and Hickerson, the right guard. Hickerson pulls and blocks the linebacker either in or out, a difficult assignment because of the angle. Wooten pulls and leads around the end, turning to the inside to wipe out any pursuer as Kelly makes his turn upfield. This is a play the Browns often use on short yardage, third and two, or on a first and ten.

The Browns have two exceptionally fine receivers in Paul Warfield, their split end, and Gary Collins at flanker. Warfield is extremely dangerous in that he has blazing speed and good broken-field running ability once he has the ball.

The Browns attempt to capitalize on both with the following play.

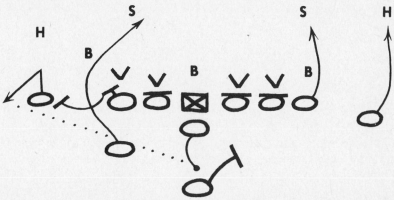

In this play the idea is to get the ball to Warfield, who has taken a couple of steps upfield and then cut back. Ryan will hit him quickly, and the tackle who has pulled along the line of scrimmage is assigned to block the defensive corner back, the one man who can stop the play before Warfield can get under way. It is effective because it makes the corner back play Warfield tighter than he'd like to, and so makes Warfield's deep patterns that much easier.

The Browns run from several flanker formations, and are very successful, mainly because Ernie Green is an exceptionally fine receiver. They will use the flanker formations in any situation, and while their big game from this formation is the pass, they will also use the pitchout and draw to Leroy Kelly.

In clutch situations (third and long yardage), look for Ryan to go to Gary Collins, principally on down-and-in patterns such as the following.

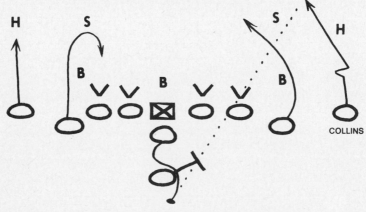

Collins is big and strong, and while he isn't the fastest around, he has a habit of coming down with the ball in a crowd. After Collins runs several of the above patterns, he has a takeoff that he also likes.

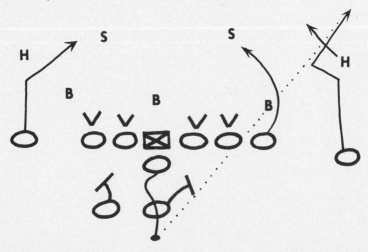

On this pattern, Collins drives down on the corner back, fakes his down-and-in, and breaks sharply to the outside. The corner back, if he has no help, such as when the Browns are in the double flanker, must respect Collins' drive to the inside and so is extremely vulnerable to this pattern.

On defense, the Browns are considered conservative but effective. They will sacrifice the short pass, but you seldom see their secondary men, Erich Barnes and Ernie Kellerman at the corners, and Ross Fichtner and Mike Howell at the safeties, beaten deep. Barnes is the best of the group at man-to-man coverage, and most quarterbacks know the best place to attack Barnes (an old teammate of mine) is to the inside on square-ins and down-and-ins.

The Browns' basic defensive philosophy is not to give up the big score — they're hard to beat deep — but they can be beaten with the pass on slant-ins and patterns short over the middle. They are not a big red-dogging defense, preferring to have their linebackers help their secondary in the pass coverage rather than getting involved in the pass rush. Their principal defense is the four-three, with Paul Wiggin and Jim Kanicki the men you must keep away from your passer if you want to throw the ball.

CLEVELAND BROWNS   1968 Veterans Roster

NO.	NAME	POS.	HT.	WT.	AGE	YRS. IN NFL	COLLEGE
52	Andrews, Bill	LB	6-½	225	23	2	Southeastern Louisiana
40	Barnes, Erich	DB	6-3	212	33	11	Purdue
87	Barney, Eppie	FL	6-0	204	23	2	Iowa State
37	Bradshaw, Jim	DB	6-2	205	29	6	Chattanooga
73	Clark, Monte	T	6-6	250	31	10	Southern California
86	Collins, Gary	FL	6-4	220	28	7	Maryland
35	Conjar, Larry	RB	6-0	214	22	2	Notre Dame
64	Copeland, James	G	6-2	245	23	2	Virginia
28	Davis, Ben	DB	5-11	185	23	2	Defiance
55	Demarie, John	T	6-3	255	23	2	LSU
88	Duncan, Ron	TE	6-5	243	25	2	Wittenberg
20	Fichtner, Ross	DB	6-0	195	29	9	Purdue
80	Glass, Bill	DE	6-5	260	33	11	Baylor
48	Green, Ernie	RB	6-2	212	29	7	Louisville
43	Green, Ron	E	6-1	200	24	2	North Dakota
81	Gregory, Jack	DE	6-5½	250	23	2	Delta State
76	Groza, Lou	PK	6-3	265	44	18	Ohio State
31	Harraway, Charley	RB	6-2	215	24	3	San Jose State
66	Hickerson, Gene	G	6-3	260	32	11	Mississippi
53	Hoaglin, Fred	C	6-4	250	24	3	Pittsburgh
82	Houston, Jim	LB	6-3	240	30	9	Ohio State
34	Howell, Mike	DB	6-1	190	25	4	Grambling
71	Johnson, Walter	DT	6-4	275	25	4	California State (L.A.)
69	Kanicki, Jim	DT	6-4	270	26	6	Michigan State
24	Kellermann, Ernie	DB	6-0	185	24	3	Miami (Ohio)
44	Kelly, Leroy	RB	6-0	200	26	5	Morgan State
15	Lane, Gary	QB	6-1	215	25	3	Missouri

NO.	NAME	POS.	HT.	WT.	AGE	YRS. IN NFL	COLLEGE
51	Lindsey, Dale	LB	6-2½	230	25	4	Western Kentucky
56	Matheson, Bob	LB	6-4	240	23	2	Duke
85	McNeil, Clifton	FL	6-2	185	28	5	Grambling
89	Morin, Milt	TE	6-4	250	25	3	Massachusetts
16	Nelsen, Bill	QB	6-0	195	27	6	Southern California
36	Pietrosante, Nick	RB	6-1	225	31	10	Notre Dame
13	Ryan, Frank	QB	6-3	207	32	11	Rice
77	Schafrath, Dick	T	6-3	248	31	10	Ohio State
41	Smith, Ralph	TE	6-2	215	29	7	Mississippi
62	Taffoni, Joe	G	6-3	250	23	2	Tennessee (Martin)
27	Ward, Carl	DB	5-9	180	24	2	Michigan
42	Warfield, Paul	E	6-0	188	25	5	Ohio State
60	Wooten, John	G	6-3	250	31	10	Colorado

CLEVELAND BROWNS 1968 Top Rookies

NAME	POS.	HT.	WT.	AGE	COLLEGE	HOW ACQUIRED*
Garlington, John	L B	6-1	225	21	Louisiana State	D-2
Meylan, Wayne	L B	6-1	239	21	Nebraska	D-4
Mitchell, Alvin	D B	6-3	195	24	Morgan State	D-10
Morrison, Reece	R B	6-0	205	22	Southwest Texas	D-3
Olszewski, Harry	G	6-0	244	21	Clemson	D-3
Upshaw, Marvin	D E	6-3	245	21	Trinity U.	D-1

*D—Draft (Number indicates draft round)
FA—Free Agent

CLEVELAND BROWNS 1968 Schedule

Sept. 15—at New Orleans	1:30		Nov. 3—at San Francisco	1:00
Sept. 22—at Dallas	1:30		Nov. 10—New Orleans	1:30
Sept. 29—Los Angeles	1:30		Nov. 17—at Pittsburgh	1:15
Oct. 5—Pittsburgh	8:30		Nov. 24—Philadelphia	1:30
Oct. 13—St. Louis	1:30		Dec. 1—New York	1:30
Oct. 20—at Baltimore	2:00		Dec. 8—at Washington	1:15
Oct. 27—Atlanta	1:30		Dec. 14—at St. Louis	1:00

NEW ORLEANS SAINTS

The New Orleans Saints, the most recent product of NFL expansion, have become the darlings of the South.

In their initial year, the Saints set attendance marks that, while expected by Louisianans, shocked the rest of the sporting world. They also played a brand of football that shocked a lot of long-established NFL teams.

They weren't expected to do much more than show up in their first year, yet they wound up winning three games and were rarely humiliated even when playing the best.

This year, confidence is a big ingredient in Tom Fears's "Machine," confidence in the knowledge they have personnel that, while not the most publicized, can do the job.

The Saints could really be termed the "extra-effort" team of the league. And nowhere was this more apparent than on defense. Brian Schweda and Mike Tilleman in the defensive line came through with top-flight performances that should be bolstered this year by the rookie efforts of Notre Dame's All-American Kevin Hardy.

The linebackers, Fred Whittingham in the middle, Steve Stonebreaker, and Ted Davis should also be stronger as the year progresses, and improvements in both these areas should help a secondary that was surprisingly effective in its first year.

The veteran Dave Whitsell heads this contingent, and last year, playing in his tenth NFL season, he tied for the lead in number of interceptions with ten.

The offense is where the Saints need basic improvements. Gary Cuozzo has moved on to Minnesota, indicating that Fears is going to go all the way with Billy Kilmer, backed up by Gary Wood and rookie Ronnie South.

Kilmer isn't by any means the prettiest passer around. As a matter of fact, his teammates kid him constantly about a ball that often appears to travel end over end. Nevertheless, he is effective and, playing with a young team, his ability to scramble is not only an asset but one that's necessary for preservation of life and limb.

Kilmer and the Saints came up with a real sleeper last year in split end Dan Abramowicz. As a rookie, Abramowicz latched onto 50 passes, many

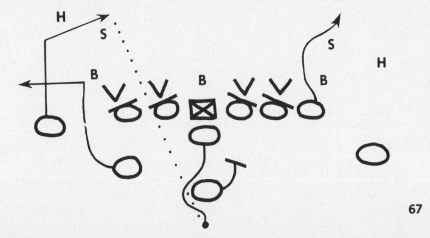

of them in nearly every one of their ball games. He's good both short and deep, and works good combinations with the halfback on the weak side.

The Saints' running game must be strengthened before they are going to improve by much over 1967. True, they have such names as Ernie Wheelwright and Jimmy Taylor, but these two big men need at least the minimal running room, or they can never get started. Here is where Tom Fears hopes he has bolstered his team the most. Eli Strand and Del Williams appear to be two fine blocking guards, and Joe Wendryhoski at center give the Saints a fairly solid middle.

Jerry Strum and Jerry Jones are also adequate at the tackle position, but all of the above are going to have to fight off rookies Dan Sartin, Ray Phillips, Dick Swatland, Joe Blake, Ellie Chattas, and possibly even Kevin Hardy.

What the Saints like to do is very similar to the Green Bay Packers' offense. They have, as I mentioned, two big backs in Taylor and Wheelwright, and also Randy Schultz, who will be difficult to keep out of the backfield if he can steer clear of the injuries which plagued him last year. One play which the Saints like in key third-and-short situations is the weak-side slant.

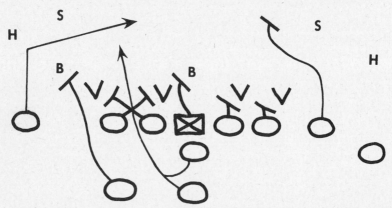

Summing up the New Orleans Saints, they have a lot of scattered talent that, if all healthy at once, can compete with any team in football. They'll need steady improvement in their offensive line and another big year from performers like Kilmer, Schweda, and Abramowicz if they are going to move up in the standings.

NEW ORLEANS SAINTS   1968 Veterans Roster

NO.	NAME	POS.	HT.	WT.	AGE	YRS. IN NFL	COLLEGE
46	Abramowicz, Dan	SE	6-1	197	23	2	Xavier (Ohio)
81	Atkins, Doug	DE	6-8	270	38	16	Tennessee
32	Barrington, Tom	RB	6-1	213	24	4	Ohio State
22	Brown, Charlie	RB	5-10	196	22	2	Missouri
83	Burke, Vern	TE	6-4	215	27	4	Oregon State
55	Burkett, Jackie	LB	6-4	228	31	8	Auburn
16	Burris, James Bo	DB	6-3	195	23	2	Houston
66	Cody, Bill	LB	6-1	227	24	3	Auburn
86	Colchico, Dan	DE	6-4	245	29	7	San Jose State

NO.	NAME	POS.	HT.	WT.	AGE	YRS. IN NFL	COLLEGE
79	Cordileone, Lou	DT	6-0	255	30	5	Clemson
47	Cortez, Bruce	DB	6-0	175	22	2	Parsons College
35	Davis, Ted	LB	6-1	232	26	5	Georgia Tech
21	Douglas, John	DB	6-1	195	23	2	Texas Southern
10	Durkee, Charlie	K	5-11	165	24	2	Oklahoma State
80	Garcia, Jim	DE	6-4	250	24	4	Purdue
42	Gilliam, John	SE	6-1	190	23	2	S. Carolina State
26	Heidel, Jim	DB	6-1	185	24	3	Mississippi
84	Hester, Jim	TE	6-4	235	23	2	North Dakota
78	Jones, Jerry	T	6-4	265	24	3	Bowling Green
30	Kelley, Les	LB	6-3	233	23	2	Alabama
17	Kilmer, Bill	QB	6-0	205	28	7	UCLA
89	Kramer, Kent	TE	6-4	235	24	3	Minnesota
50	Kupp, Jake	G	6-3	233	27	5	Washington
72	Leggett, Earl	DT	6-3	265	34	11	LSU
0	Logan, Obert	DB	5-10	180	26	4	Trinity (Texas)
36	McCall, Don	RB	5-11	195	23	2	Southern California
75	McCormick, Dave	T	6-6	250	25	3	LSU
12	McNeill, Tom	Punt	6-1	195	26	2	Stephen F. Austin
24	Nevett, Elijah	FL	6-0	185	24	2	Clark College
85	Poage, Ray	FL	6-3	205	27	5	Texas
77	Rissmiller, Ray	T	6-4	250	26	3	Georgia
27	Roberts, Walter	FL	5-10	163	26	5	San Jose State
44	Rose, George	DB	5-11	190	26	5	Auburn
76	Rowe, Dave	DT	6-6	280	23	2	Penn State
63	Schmidt, Roy	G	6-3	250	26	2	Long Beach State
33	Schultz, Randy	RB	6-0	210	24	3	State College of Iowa
60	Schweda, Brian	DE	6-3	250	25	3	Kansas
53	Simmons, Dave	LB	6-4	245	25	4	Georgia Tech
37	Stonebreaker, Steve	LB	6-3	225	29	6	Detroit
58	Strand, Eli	G	6-2	250	25	3	Iowa State
73	Sturm, Jerry	T	6-3	265	31	2*	Illinois
71	Sutton, Archie	T	6-4	265	26	4	Illinois
31	Taylor, Jim	RB	6-0	220	32	11	LSU
74	Tilleman, Mike	DT	6-6	280	24	3	Montana
54	Wendryhoski, Joe	C	6-2	245	28	5	Illinois
23	Whitsell, Dave	DB	6-0	185	32	11	Indiana
59	Whittingham, Fred	LB	6-2	240	28	4	California Poly
39	Wheelwright, Ernie	RB	6-3	236	28	5	Southern Illinois
61	Williams, Del	G	6-2	240	22	2	Florida State
19	Wood, Gary	QB	5-11	188	26	5	Cornell
20	Youngblood, George	DB	6-3	205	23	3	Los Angeles State

*Player has additional years pro experience in AFL.

NEW ORLEANS SAINTS   1968 Top Rookies

NAME	POS.	HT.	WT.	AGE	COLLEGE	HOW ACQUIRED*
Blake, Joe	G	6-2	278	23	Tulsa	D-9
Crittendon, Willie	DT	6-5	275	23	Tulsa	D-4
Hardy, Kevin	DE	6-5	275	21	Notre Dame	D-1
Howard, Eugene	DB	6-0	190	21	Langston	D-7
Jackson, Bob	RB	6-3	245	27	New Mexico State	FA
Phillips, Ray	G	6-3	245	22	Michigan	D-7
Sartin, Dan	G	6-2	230	22	Mississippi	D-4 (Dall.)
South, Ronnie Lee	QB-K	6-1	195	23	Arkansas	D-5

NAME	POS.	HT.	WT.	AGE	COLLEGE	HOW ACQUIRED*
Swatland, Dick	G	6-1	240	22	Notre Dame	D-8
Szymakowski, Dave	FL	6-2	198	22	West Texas State	D-3

*D— Draft (Number indicates draft round)
FA— Free Agent

NEW ORLEANS SAINTS 1968 Schedule

Sept. 15—Cleveland	1:30		Nov. 3—Dallas	1:00
Sept. 22—Washington	1:30		Nov. 10—at Cleveland	1:30
Sept. 29—St. Louis	1:30		Nov. 17—Green Bay (Milwaukee)	1:00
Oct. 6—at New York	1:30		Nov. 24—at Detroit	1:15
Oct. 13—Minnesota	1:30		Dec. 1—Chicago	1:00
Oct. 20—at Pittsburgh	1:30		Dec. 8—at Philadelphia	1:15
Oct. 27—at St. Louis	1:00		Dec. 15—Pittsburgh	1:00

PITTSBURGH STEELERS

Steeler head coach Bill Austin is a former teammate of mine, going back to when we both worked at the Polo Grounds for the New York Giants.

That's incidental to the fact that he also learned a lot of football from the same man as I did, Vince Lombardi. Bill not only played under Vince, but he later coached under Lombardi, and consequently his approach to the game is very similar. Both agree it is a game of violence. Austin says, "To become great, a player must have complete dedication, and he must be willing to pay the price if he wishes to become great."

As a player, I can vouch for the fact that Bill paid the price in full. He wasn't one of the biggest offensive guards, but through work and dedication he became one of the best.

Bill thinks the Steelers should be able to play on a par with any team in football in 1968. By trading his starting quarterback of last year, Bill Nelsen, Austin has indicated that he is thoroughly satisfied that Kent Nix is more than capable of handling that all-important position. Nix showed a remarkable amount of cool last year in his first starting role, and also displayed a first-rate arm for both the short and the deep pass.

He has a good corps of receivers, headed by Roy Jefferson, who was hampered last year by injuries, and J. R. Wilburn. Jefferson is a top all-around football player who has found a home on the flank. His best pass route is deep across the middle, but he also runs all the short patterns necessary for third-down ball-control situations.

John Hilton is another fine receiver, whom Nix likes to use on the square-out to the flanker side, on third-and-long situations.

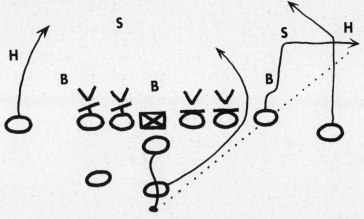

Hilton is also adept at the turn-in pass that Green Bay uses so frequently.

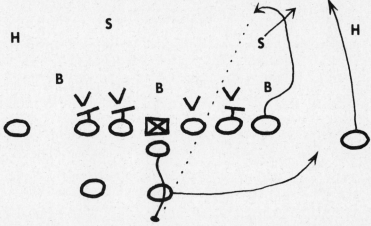

The Steelers' running game has been bolstered by Don Shy and the improvement last year of Earl Gros. Gros has the same background as Austin, in that he played for Green Bay before traveling to Philadelphia. His big move is the weak-side off-tackle play the Steelers use on short yardage situations.

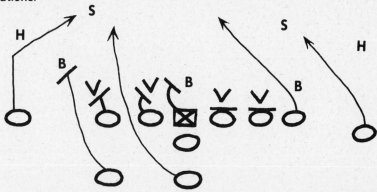

Operating with Gros and Shy in the Steelers' ground game is Dick Hoak. Hoak, while not particularly fast, is a very productive runner who handles the "Green Bay" power sweep in good shape and also runs well with the off-tackle takeoff on the sweep, used on third and short.

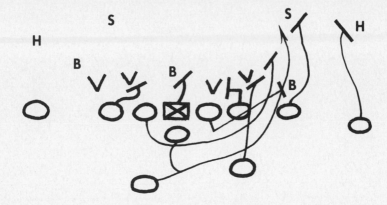

Hoak also gives the Steelers a strong threat with the run-pass option play.

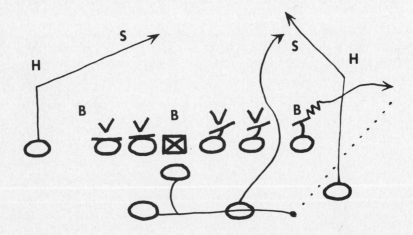

Defensively, the Steelers do not have to back away from any team. Their front four, in a basic four-three most of the time, is big and strong and well supported by linebackers Andy Russell, John Campbell, and Bill Saul.

The Steelers really stand out in their defensive secondary. Safety men Paul Martha and Clendon Thomas and left corner back Marv Woodson are excellent on the man-to-man coverage which Austin's four-three calls for. Watch Woodson on his man-to-man play, as he is one of the best in the league.

In summation, the Steelers, as they always have been, are a rough football team. Bill Austin's demands for dedication are being met and the Steelers, definitely on the way up, can win against the best.

PITTSBURGH STEELERS   1968 Veterans Roster

NO.	NAME	POS.	HT.	WT.	AGE	YRS. IN NFL	COLLEGE
46	Anderson, Chet	TE	6-3	245	23	2	Minnesota
71	Arndt, Dick	DT	6-5	265	24	2	Idaho
30	Asbury, Bill	FB	6-1	225	25	3	Kent State
11	Badar, Rich	QB	6-1	190	25	2	Indiana
74	Brown, John	T	6-2	255	29	7	Syracuse
23	Butler, Jim	HB	5-10	192	25	4	Edward Waters
53	Campbell, John	LB	6-3	225	29	6	Minnesota
83	Clark, Mike	K	6-2	210	27	6	Texas A&M
45	Compton, Dick	E	6-1	195	28	5	McMurry College
89	Cropper, Marshall	E	6-3	200	24	2	Maryland State
57	Davis, Sam	G	6-1	245	24	2	Allen U.
6	Elliott, Jim	P	5-11	185	25	2	Presbyterian
9	Foruria, John	DB	6-2	205	23	2	Idaho State
79	Gagner, Larry	G	6-3	249	24	3	Florida
38	Gros, Earl	FB	6-3	220	28	7	LSU
76	Haggerty, Mike	T	6-4	241	22	2	Miami (Fla.)
67	Hilgenberg, Wally	LB	6-3	235	25	4	Iowa
82	Hilton, John	TE	6-5	222	26	4	Richmond
64	Hinton, Chuck	DT	6-5	258	29	5	N. Carolina College
42	Hoak, Dick	HB	5-11	195	28	8	Penn State
29	Hohn, Bob	DB	6-0	185	27	4	Nebraska
87	Jefferson, Roy	FL	6-2	190	24	4	Utah
84	Jeter, Tony	TE	6-3	223	23	2	Nebraska
75	Kortas, Ken	DT	6-4	280	26	5	Louisville
60	McGee, Ben	DE	6-3	250	29	5	Jackson State
68	Magac, Mike	G	6-3	240	30	9	Missouri
73	Mansfield, Ray	C	6-3	240	27	6	Washington
85	Marion, Jerry	E	5-11	185	24	2	Wyoming
20	Martha, Paul	DB	6-0	187	26	5	Pittsburgh
59	May, Ray	LB	6-1	230	23	2	Southern California
61	Mazzanti, Jerry	DE	6-2	242	28	4	Arkansas
37	Morgan, Bob	DB	6-0	205	28	2	New Mexico
10	Nix, Kent	QB	6-2	195	24	2	TCU
72	O'Brien, Fran	T	6-1	265	32	10	Michigan State
78	Parker, Frank	DT	6-5	270	28	6	Oklahoma State
34	Russell, Andy	LB	6-2	225	26	4	Missouri
50	Saul, Bill,	LB	6-4	232	27	6	Penn State
17	Shiner, Dick	QB	6-0	197	25	5	Maryland
25	Shy, Don	HB	6-1	205	22	2	San Diego State
28	Thomas, Clendon	DB	6-2	200	32	11	Oklahoma
66	Van Dyke, Bruce	G	6-2	246	24	3	Missouri
65	Voss, Lloyd	DE	6-4	256	26	5	Nebraska
62	Wenzel, Ralph	G	6-2	236	25	3	San Diego State
86	Wilburn, J. R.	E	6-2	190	25	3	South Carolina
—	Whitlow, Bob	C	6-2	238	32	7	Arizona
47	Woodson, Marv	DB	6-0	195	27	5	Indiana

PITTSBURGH STEELERS   1968 Top Rookies

NAME	POS.	HT.	WT.	AGE	COLLEGE	HOW ACQUIRED*
Dalton, Doug	FB	6-1	207	22	New Mexico State	D-7
Glennon, Bill	T	6-2	235	22	Washington	D-7 (L.A.)
Hebert, Ken	E-K	6-0	200	22	Houston	D-3 (L.A.)

NAME	POS.	HT.	WT.	AGE	COLLEGE	HOW ACQUIRED*
Henderson, Jon	D B	6-0	195	23	Colorado State	D-3
Ruple, Ernie	T	6-4	256	22	Arkansas	D-2
Taylor, Mike	T	6-4	246	20	Southern California	D-1

*D—Draft (Number indicates draft round)
FA—Free Agent

PITTSBURGH STEELERS   1968 Schedule

Sept. 15—New York	1:30		Nov. 3—at Atlanta	1:15
Sept. 22—at Los Angeles	1:00		Nov.10—at St. Louis	1:00
Sept. 29—Baltimore	1:30		Nov. 17—Cleveland	1:15
Oct. 5—at Cleveland	8:30		Nov. 24—San Francisco	1:15
Oct. 13—at Washington	1:30		Dec. 1—St. Louis	1:15
Oct. 20—New Orleans	1:30		Dec. 8—at Dallas	1:00
Oct. 27—Philadelphia	1:30		Dec. 15—at New Orleans	1:00

ST. LOUIS CARDINALS

The St. Louis Cardinals went into last season as one of the top contenders for divisional honors, only to see their chances destroyed before the season even got under way. Quarterback Charlie Johnson was called to the service, as was linebacker Larry Stallings, and while coach Charlie Winner reshuffled accordingly, the Cards, also heavily hit by injuries, never really got started.

This year, there should be much more stability to the Cards. Young Jim Hart emerged from the chaos that developed with the loss of quarterback Johnson and seemingly improved with every performance. While at times throwing with the best in the game, Hart suffered heavily from interceptions. Last year, he was "picked off" 30 times, but this year, after a season of looking at defenses, much improvement is expected.

Dave Williams, also a rookie last year, is another bright spot for the Cards. Williams, like Hart, came on fast, and wound up the season with 28 catches, good for 405 yards and 5 touchdowns.

Bobby Joe Conrad, last year's leading receiver, and halfback Johnny Roland, coming off knee surgery, can again be counted on to add stability to the Cardinals' offense. The lack of Roland and Conrad put so much of the pressure on what I think is one of the best defensive teams in the game.

They red-dog linebackers at any time and in any situation. They also are best at the safety blitz, one reason being that they have the best all-around safety man in the game, Larry Wilson. But it doesn't end there. The entire Cardinal defense knows one speed, and that's all-out.

These are two of the Cardinals' safety blitzes, which they first used in 1961.

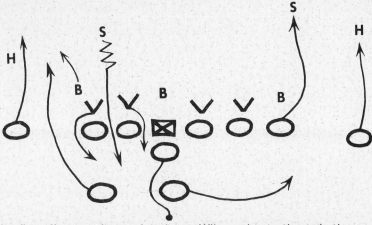

In the first diagram, free safety Larry Wilson shoots through the gap between his defensive end and tackle. His man-to-man assignment against the

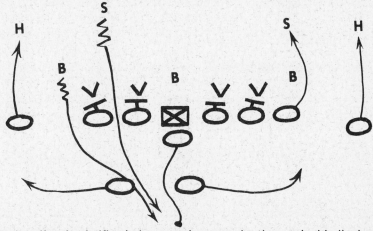

pass, the offensive halfback, is now taken over by the weak-side linebacker. This is a defense the Cards will come with at any time, and it is dangerous for the Cards because all of the deep secondary men are now without help, and stuck with man-to-man situations on the flanker, the tight end, and the split end. In other words, the Cards bank on getting to the passer before a receiver has time to work himself into the clear.

In the second diagram, the Cards have sent both the weak-side linebacker and Larry Wilson, and unless the offensive team has anticipated this defense and kept their set backs in, there are not enough blockers to handle the rush. In other words, six men are rushing and only five remain to block.

The Cards' defensive skill is not all wrapped up in the red-dog. Corner backs Pat Fischer and Jim Burson are stick-outs at man-to-man coverage. Jerry Stovall has developed into one of the league's best tight safeties, and of course there is Wilson, who is in a class by himself. They work extremely well together, as does the defensive line headed by veterans Don Brumm, Sam Silas, and Chuck Walker. At the middle-linebacker spot is possibly the league's most underrated linebacker, Dale Meinert. He's the key to the varied fronts with which the Cards' defense confuses the opposition's blocking assignments. He moves in and out of the line, before the snap of the ball, and can cover deep on the pass as effectively as he can become a pass rusher. It is a solid defensive team, and one most quarterbacks would like to pass up.

On the offense, Johnny Roland has given the Cards the spark of a championship team. The 1966 NFL Rookie of the Year is a great broken-field runner, an excellent pass receiver, and can, if called upon, throw the option pass.

The Cards' game, however, even with Roland's running ability, is a passing one. Quarterback Hart has four top receivers in split end Dave Williams, tight end Jackie Smith, flanker Bobby Joe Conrad, and Billy Gambrell, who plays both flanker and split end. Hart's best game is a short one, and on third-down "must" passes, he likes to work simple individual patterns to Conrad.

Williams is better on the down-and-in, while Conrad runs a very good square-out. The depths of these patterns are called by Hart in the huddle, depending upon the yardage needed. These are two of the pass plays you can look for. The first is a flat pass to Roland similar to a screen pass that is used to get Roland into an open field. He generally does the rest.

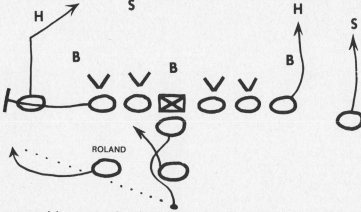

The second is a pass that Hart likes to throw and Conrad likes to run. You can almost set your clock on this one when the Cards have moved inside their opponent's 30-yard line, and have a first and ten, or a third and long yardage.

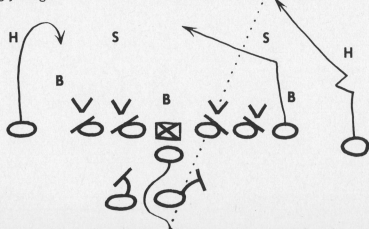

The Cards' running game, because of their frequent use of the pass, is designed to take advantage of the defense's pass rush.

They use the draw play extensively, and at any time. They also like this trap play, with Roland hitting quickly into the middle.

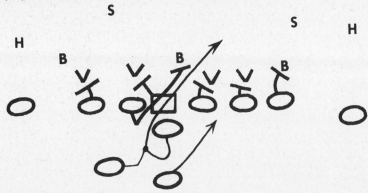

In summation, the cards are a passing team on offense, a hard-nosed red-dogging team on defense. And if they can stay healthy, they are the equal of any team in the NFL.

ST. LOUIS CARDINALS   1968 Veterans Roster

NO.	NAME	POS.	HT.	WT.	AGE	YRS. IN NFL	COLLEGE
25	Bakken, Jim	K-FL	6-0	200	27	7	Wisconsin
20	Barnes, Mike	DB	6-3	205	23	2	Arlington State
65	Battle, Jim	DE-DT	6-3	250	27	2	Southern U.
86	Brumm, Don	DE	6-3	245	26	6	Purdue
30	Bryant, Charlie	RB	5-11	205	27	3	Allen U. (S.C.)
—	Clark, Ernie	LB	6-1	230	31	6	Michigan State
40	Conrad, Bobby Joe	FL	6-2	195	32	11	Texas A&M
33	Crenshaw, Willis	RB	6-1	230	27	5	Kansas State
61	DeMarco, Bob	C	6-2	240	29	8	Dayton
3	Gambrell, Billy	E	5-10	175	26	6	South Carolina
55	Goode, Irv	G-C	6-5	250	27	7	Kentucky
64	Gray, Ken	G	6-2	250	32	11	Howard Payne
17	Hart, Jim	QB	6-2	205	24	3	Southern Illinois
74	Heron, Fred	DE	6-4	260	23	3	San Jose State
87	Hillebrand, Jerry	LB	6-3	240	28	6	Colorado
12	Johnson, Charley	QB	6-0	190	29	8	New Mexico State
51	Kasperek, Dick	C	6-3	250	25	3	Iowa State
26	Latourette, Chuck	P-DB	6-0	190	23	2	Rice
83	Logan, Chuck	E	6-4	220	25	4	Northwestern
89	Long, Dave	DT	6-4	255	23	3	Iowa
73	McMillan, Ernie	T	6-6	260	30	8	Illinois
60	Meggyesy, Dave	LB	6-1	230	26	6	Syracuse
62	Meinert, Dale	LB	6-3	225	34	11	Oklahoma
52	O'Brien, Dave	G-T	6-2	245	27	6	Boston College
71	Reynolds, Bob	T	6-5	265	29	6	Bowling Green
23	Roland, John	RB	6-2	210	25	3	Missouri
75	Rowe, Bob	DE	6-4	260	23	2	Western Michigan
42	Sanders, Lonnie	DB	6-3	207	26	6	Michigan State
27	Shivers, Ron	RB	5-11	200	26	3	Utah State
72	Silas, Sam	DT	6-4	250	27	6	Southern Illinois

NO.	NAME	POS.	HT.	WT.	AGE	YRS. IN NFL	COLLEGE
81	Smith, Jackie	E	6-4	225	28	6	N.W.Louisiana
66	Sortun, Rick	G	6-2	235	25	5	Washington
19	Spiller, Phil	DB	6-0	195	23	2	Los Angeles State
67	Stallings, Larry	LB	6-2	230	26	6	Georgia Tech
21	Stovall, Jerry	DB	6-2	195	27	6	LSU
57	Strofolino, Mike	LB	6-2	230	24	4	Villanova
79	Walker, Chuck	DT	6-3	245	27	5	Duke
82	Wheeler, Ted	E	6-3	235	22	2	West Texas State
45	Williams, Bobby	DB	6-0	200	26	3	Central State (Okla.)
63	Williams, Clyde	T	6-2	255	28	2	Southern U.
80	Williams, Dave	FL	6-2	205	23	2	Washington
8	Wilson, Larry	DB	6-0	190	30	9	Utah

ST. LOUIS CARDINALS 1968 Top Rookies

NAME	POS.	HT.	WT.	AGE	COLLEGE	HOW ACQUIRED*
Atkins, Robert	D B	6-3	212	21	Grambling	D-2
Campbell, Mike	R B	5-11	200	23	Lenoir Rhyne	D-6, '67
Edwards, Cid	R B	6-2	230	24	Tennessee A & I	FA
Hyatt, Fred	F L	6-3	212	21	Auburn	D-2
Lawe, MacArthur	R B	6-0	220	24	Utah State	D-1
Rivers, Jamie	L B	6-2	235	22	Bowling Green	D-5, '67
Wosilius, Bill	L B-DE	6-5	235	22	Syracuse	D-15,'67

*D — Draft (Number indicates draft round)
FA — Free Agent

ST. LOUIS CARDINALS 1968 Schedule

Sept. 16 — Los Angeles	8:30		Nov. 3 — at Philadelphia	1:15
Sept. 22 — at San Francisco	1:00		Nov. 10 — Pittsburgh	1:00
Sept. 29 — at New Orleans	1:30		Nov. 17 — at Baltimore	2:00
Oct. 6 — Dallas	1:00		Nov. 24 — Atlanta	1:00
Oct. 13 — at Cleveland	1:30		Dec. 1 — at Pittsburgh	1:15
Oct. 20 — Washington	1:00		Dec. 8 — at New York	1:30
Oct. 27 — New Orleans	1:00		Dec. 14 — Cleveland	1:00

CHICAGO BEARS

When George Halas stepped down as head coach of the Chicago Bears last May, he did so confident that he had the man to uphold the legacy of the Chicago Bears. He named Jim Dooley, a former Bears' star receiver and, more recently, a spectacularly successful assistant coach, as his replacement.

Dooley has never known another professional life other than that dispensed by George Halas, and he can be expected to carry on in the same tradition as the "Poppa" Bear.

On the field, Halas demanded 100 percent plus effort, and his players' compliance with this demand is best seen on the defense. The Bears use many defensive alignments, but, while they show the opposition many confusing fronts, they usually return to some type of gap defense. To use so many defenses requires a great deal of practice and book work, and it's been said by former Bears that Chicago leads the league in this department.

They also, to my way of thinking, lead the league in all-out effort.

The key man in the Bears' defense is middle linebacker Dick Butkus. He is everywhere at once, and is destined to become an all-time great. He is effective in the red-dog, which the Bears use a great deal, and he also possesses the speed to range far back to help the secondary. He is a sure tackler, and has the size at 250 pounds to stop a big back in his tracks.

I recall watching him perform against the Giants in his rookie year. He was involved in a red-dog, and while he narrowly missed quarterback Earl Morrall, who got the pass off, it was Butkus who seconds later came up with the receiver's fumble some 15 yards downfield.

Butkus is flanked by two linebackers, Doug Buffone and Jim Purnell, who are specialists at the red-dog, as well as fine pass defenders.

The Bears' front four and linebacking corps do many things in their complete dedication to get to the opposition's passer. One of the maneuvers that Bear linemen will use in the pass rush is the following.

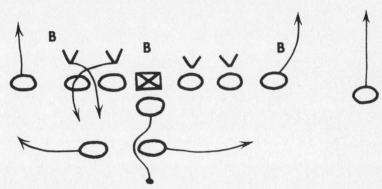

As you can see, when the end and the tackle exchange pass-rush alleys it can apply a lot of pressure on a blocking lineman. If either the offensive guard or tackle makes a mistake, it means trouble for the quarterback from either the Bear end or tackle.

The front four, led by Dick Evey and Frank Cornish, can get away with these maneuvers because of the strength of the linebackers behind them.

For a similar reason (the strength of the Bears' four deep secondary), the Bears' linebackers can also take more than an occasional risk on the dog, in a calculated guess of the coming play.

The Bears' four-man deep has great speed, with safeties Richie Petitbon and Rosie Taylor — two men with the range and speed to cause trouble for most enemy quarterbacks.

When watching the Bears' defense, look for some rather strange front-line alignments that usually shift back to a gap defense at the snap of the ball. Watch for the red-dog on second and long, and third and long. And keep an eye on Butkus; he's everywhere.

Offensively, the Bears can be summed up in a word, Sayers. Gale Sayers does a little bit of everything. In three years, Sayers has gained nearly 3,000 yards rushing, caught 79 passes, and returned eight kickoffs and punt returns for touchdowns.

Last year, Jack Concannon also added to the Bears' offense with a scrambling type of quarterback play that should be improved now with a year's playing time under his belt.

Still, no matter how you cut it, the Bears' offense is Gale Sayers, and the Bears do many things to get him into a position to use his incredible broken-field running skill.

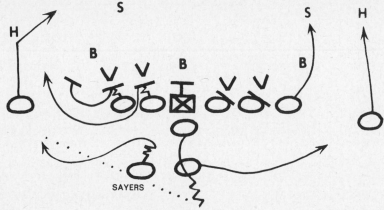

Above is a screen pass to Sayers designed to get him into the open field where he can use one or more blockers.

This is a takeoff on the screen and is really a flare pass with the tackle pulling and becoming a blocker for Sayers.

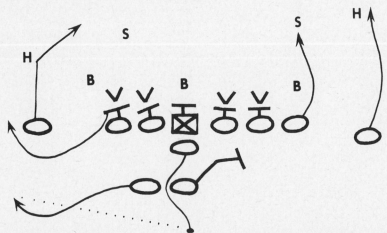

In the running game Sayers can go inside, but he is much better outside, where speed is a factor.

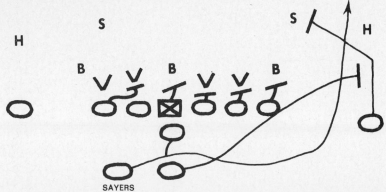

SAYERS

In watching the Bears' offense, you can look for Concannon to get the ball to Sayers as often as possible. Johnny Morris will be the prime receiver for third and long yardage, and he has a variety of patterns, the best of which is the square-out (at first-down distance), the slant-in, and the fly (straight down the field).

CHICAGO BEARS   1968 Veterans Roster

NO.	NAME	POS.	HT.	WT.	AGE	YRS. IN NFL	COLLEGE
82	Allen, Duane	TE	6-4	225	30	8	Santa Ana J.C.
81	Amsler, Marty	DE	6-5	255	25	2	Evansville
84	Becker, Wayne	C	6-7	265	23	1	Montana
27	Bristo, Fred	DB	6-0	178	24	1	Tennessee State
22	Brown, Charlie	DB	6-1	193	25	3	Syracuse
55	Buffone, Doug	LB	6-3	230	23	3	Louisville
10	Bukich, Rudy	QB	6-2	205	35	14	Southern California
29	Bull, Ron	RB	6-0	200	27	7	Baylor
51	Butkus, Dick	LB	6-3	245	25	4	Illinois
49	Butler, Floyd	RB-FL	5-6	150	27	1	N.E. Oklahoma
72	Cadile, Jim	G	6-3	240	27	7	San Jose State
15	Carter, Virgil	QB	6-1	185	22	1	Brigham Young
11	Concannon, Jack	QB	6-3	205	24	5	Boston College
73	Cornish, Frank	DT	6-6	285	23	3	Grambling
61	Croftcheck, Don	G	6-1	230	25	4	Indiana
84	Denney, Austin	TE	6-2	229	23	2	Tennessee
23	Dodd, Al	DB	6-0	180	22	2	N.W. Louisiana
79	Evey, Dick	DT	6-4	245	26	5	Tennessee
83	Francis, Ron	TE	6-5	226	24	1	North Carolina A & T
46	Gentry, Curtiss	DB	6-0	185	26	3	Maryland State
45	Gordon, Dick	SE	5-11	190	24	3	Michigan State
88	Green, Bobby Joe	P	5-11	175	31	9	Florida
25	Greenlee, Tom	DB	6-0	205	22	1	Washington
65	Jackson, Randy	T	6-5	245	23	2	Florida
76	Johnson, John	DT	6-5	260	26	6	Indiana
43	Jones, Bob	FL	6-4	196	22	2	San Diego State
80	Jones, Jimmy	SE	6-2	187	26	4	Wisconsin
71	Kollmann, Jim	G	6-3	230	23	1	Oregon
60	Kriewald, Doug	G	6-4	245	22	2	West Texas State
59	Kuechenberg, Rudy	LB	6-2	215	24	2	Purdue
32	Kurek, Ralph	FB	6-2	210	24	4	Wisconsin
48	Livingston, Andy	FB	6-1	230	23	5	Phoenix, J.C.
44	Lyle, Garry	RB	6-2	198	22	1	George Washington
26	McRae, Bennie	DB	6-0	180	28	7	Michigan State

NO.	NAME	POS.	HT.	WT.	AGE	YRS. IN NFL	COLLEGE
58	McRae, Franklin	DE	6-6½	270	23	2	Tennessee State
47	Morris, Johnny	FL	5-10	180	31	11	U.C. Santa Barbara
87	O'Bradovich, Ed	DE	6-3	255	27	7	Illinois
83	Percival, Mac	PK	6-4	220	27	2	Texas Tech
17	Petitbon, Richie	DB	6-3	208	29	10	Tulane
86	Phillips, Loyd	DE	6-3	240	22	2	Arkansas
41	Piccolo, Brian	RB	6-0	205	24	4	Wake Forest
70	Pickens, Bob	T	6-4	258	24	2	Nebraska
53	Purnell, Jim	LB	6-2	238	26	5	Wisconsin
50	Pyle, Mike	C	6-3	250	28	8	Yale
12	Rakestraw, Larry	QB	6-2	195	25	5	Georgia
62	Reilly, Mike	LB	6-2½	238	25	5	Iowa
40	Sayers, Gale	RB	6-0	198	24	4	Kansas
67	Seals, George	G	6-3	260	25	5	Missouri
20	Taylor, Joe	DB	6-1	200	27	2	North Carolina A&T
24	Taylor, Roosevelt	DB	5-11	186	30	8	Grambling
63	Wetoska, Bob	T	6-3	240	30	9	Notre Dame

CHICAGO BEARS   1968 Top Rookies

NAME	POS.	HT.	WT.	AGE	COLLEGE	HOW ACQUIRED*
Hull, Mike	R B	6-3½	220	22	Southern California	D-1
Wallace, Bob	F L-TE	6-3	211	22	Texas Western	D-2
Hazleton, Major	D B	6-1	185	23	Florida A&M	D-3
Turner, Cecil	F L-DB	5-10	170	22	California Poly	D-5
Schmedding, Jim	O G-C	6-2	252	21	Weber State	D-6

*D — Draft (Number indicates draft round)
FA — Free Agent

CHICAGO BEARS   1968 Schedule

Sept. 15 — Washington	1:00		Nov. 3 — at Green Bay	1:00
Sept. 22 — at Detroit	1:15		Nov. 10 — San Francisco	1:00
Sept. 29 — at Minnesota	1:30		Nov. 17 — Atlanta	1:00
Oct. 6 — at Baltimore	2:00		Nov. 24 — Dallas	1:00
Oct. 13 — Detroit	1:00		Dec. 1 — at New Orleans	1:00
Oct. 20 — at Philadelphia	1:15		Dec. 8 — at Los Angeles	1:00
Oct. 27 — Minnesota	1:00		Dec. 15 — Green Bay	1:00

DETROIT LIONS

For years the Detroit Lions were known as a team that played the game of football only one way — all-out. Through their championship years of the fifties, if they didn't beat you they certainly gave you a beating.

Something happened in the last few years to change the attitude of this team. The personnel was still there, some of the finest in the league, but the 100 percent effort was gone. When head coach Joe Schmidt took over last year, he let it be known that the "picnic" was over.

On accepting his first head coaching job after one year as an assistant, Joe stated flatly, "If one of our players won't go all out, he will soon go somewhere else. Professional football is a game of pride. A winning team must have desire. My job is to see that every Detroit Lion player possesses these attributes."

The Lions have always been a team that beats you on defense. This is understandable, because they have some of the best men ever to play the defensive game, Alex Karras and Jerry Rush, with Larry Hand and Joe Robb playing the end positions. They are strong and quick, and when they make an all-out effort they can literally destroy an opponent's inside running game.

Theoretically, no team should run much against the Lions. They have such exceptional strength on the line that most teams approach them with an attitude of "we'll have to throw the ball."

The Lions' secondary led by Lem Barney, is also well stocked, as are the linebacking positions in their four-three defense. Mike Lucci is a quick, skilled middle man, and Wayne Walker and Paul Naumoff are effective at the red-dog, against the run, and when dropping into pass coverage.

Under Joe Schmidt, the Lions have restored the red-dog to its full potential. Joe was possibly the best MLB in the business, operating from that position with the front four paving the way ahead.

The following is one of the Lions' key dogs. While they like to dog on second and long yardage, and first and ten, they will come at any time and in any

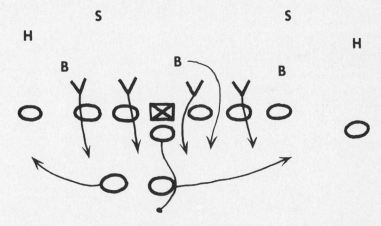

situation. The success of the above red-dog is found in Karras and Rush. They have the strength to command double-team blocking and this generally will free an area for the middle linebacker.

Another red-dog combination the Lions like is the middle linebacker and the weak-side linebacker. With pressure from Walker and Lucci on the passer, the Lions' very adequate defensive secondary can take a lot of chances on interceptions. This is true because they know that even though they are now in man-to-man coverage with little linebacking help, the quarterback is not going to have a whole lot of time to get the ball off. Last year's rookie corner back Lem Barney could reach his full potential this year.

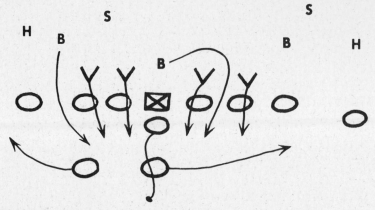

He plays very tight on a receiver, and with the return of the red-dog and the resulting wild passes, he should again be a top interceptor.

Offensively, the Lions have gained a new lease on life with the acquisition of quarterback Bill Munson from the Los Angeles Rams. Munson is a classical pro quarterback; he doesn't scramble a lot, but can throw the ball extremely well short or long. Playing behind Gabriel with the Rams (and many thought he shouldn't have), Munson may have stagnated somewhat, but he shouldn't be long in regaining the form that made him the Rams' starter in 1965.

In Ron Kramer, the tight end, Bill Malinchak, the flanker, and Gail Cogdill, the split end, the Lions have a well-rounded set of receivers. Cogdill has all the moves, deep and short. He can run a deep zig-out that is almost impossible to cover man-to-man. He runs a fly pattern and has great hands in a crowd. Ron Kramer gives the Lions the short game every passing club needs. He is exceptional working over the middle in "company," as he is so large that he can often just take it away from a smaller man.

Below is another pattern which Kramer runs well. It is often a third-and-

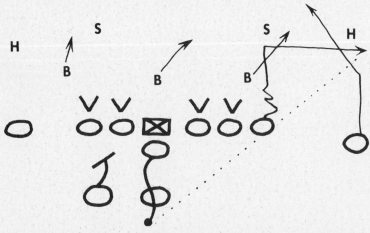

long call of the Lions. The Lions running game should be stronger than it's been in years in 1968. Mel Farr, coming off a fantastic rookie-of-the-year season, can go inside or out, and he should be complemented with the return of the injured Nick Eddy. John Gordy is perhaps the best blocking lineman, and he is used both straight ahead and pulling to lead this power

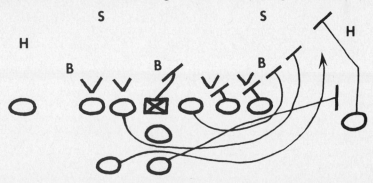

sweep. The Lions' set backs are interchangeable in that each runs from either position. Tom Nowatzke and Amos March are the strong inside threats, and Farr and Eddy will continue to develop and give the Lions the necessary outside strength.

In summation, while the Lions probably won't bounce all the way back this year, teams they meet in '68 are going to know they've been in ball games. They'll return more and more to their old style of play, which was a strong red-dogging, gambling defense, the kind that, when it plays all-out, results in interceptions and fumbles, and wins ball games.

DETROIT LIONS   1968 Veterans Roster

NO.	NAME	POS.	HT.	WT.	AGE	YRS. IN NFL	COLLEGE
50	Alford, Mike	C	6-3	235	25	3	Auburn
78	Baker, John	DE	6-6	270	32	11	N. Carolina College
20	Barney, Lem	DB	6-0	185	22	2	Jackson State
26	Bass, Mike	DB	6-0	190	22	2	Michigan
79	Bradshaw, Charlie	T	6-6	260	32	11	Baylor
89	Cogdill, Gail	E	6-2	200	31	9	Washington State
52	Cottrell, Bill	T	6-2	250	24	2	Delaware Valley
24	Farr, Mel	RB	6-1	205	23	2	UCLA
45	Felts, Bobby	RB	6-2	205	26	4	Florida A&M
54	Flanagan, Ed	C	6-3	250	24	4	Purdue
68	Gallagher, Frank	G	6-2	240	25	2	North Carolina
80	Gibbons, Jim	TE	6-3	230	32	11	Iowa
57	Goovert, Ron	LB	5-11	225	24	2	Michigan State
75	Gordy, John	G	6-4	245	33	11	Tennessee
74	Hand, Larry	DE	6-4	245	28	4	Appalachian
87	Henderson, John	E-FL	6-3	200	25	4	Michigan
85	Kamanu, Lew	DE	6-4	245	24	2	Weber State
71	Karras, Alex	DT	6-2	255	33	10	Iowa
43	Kopay, Dave	RB	6-0	225	26	5	Washington
66	Kowalkowski, Bob	G	6-3	245	24	3	Virginia
88	Kramer, Ron	TE	6-3	235	33	11	Michigan
44	LeBeau, Dick	DB	6-1	185	31	10	Ohio State

NO.	NAME	POS.	HT.	WT.	AGE	YRS. IN NFL	COLLEGE
53	Lucci, Mike	LB	6-2	230	28	7	Tennessee
21	Maher, Bruce	DB	5-11	185	30	9	Detroit
81	Malinchak, Bill	E	6-1	200	24	3	Indiana
31	Marsh, Amos	RB	6-0	225	29	8	Oregon State
86	McCambridge, John	DE	6-4	245	22	2	Northwestern
83	Melinkovich, Mike	DE	6-4	250	26	4	Gray Harbor J.C.
70	Moore, Denis	DT	6-5	255	23	2	Southern California
19	Munson, Bill	QB	6-2	200	27	5	Utah State
58	Naumoff, Paul	LB	6-1	225	23	2	Tennessee
35	Nowatzke, Tom	RB	6-3	230	26	4	Indiana
47	Rasmussen, Wayne	DB	6-2	175	26	5	S. Dakota State
—	Robb, Joe	DE	6-3	245	31	10	TCU
49	Robinson, John	DB-FL	6-3	205	23	2	Tennessee State
82	Rush, Jerry	DT	6-4	260	25	4	Michigan State
73	Shoals, Roger	T	6-4	255	29	6	Maryland
14	Sweetan, Karl	QB	6-1	200	25	3	Wake Forest
27	Thompson, Bobby	DB	5-10	185	29	5	Arizona
48	Vaughn, Tom	DB	5-11	190	25	4	Iowa State
55	Walker, Wayne	LB-K	6-2	225	30	11	Idaho
63	Walton, Chuck	G	6-3	250	27	2	Iowa State
28	Weger, Mike	DB	6-1	185	22	2	Bowling Green
77	Winkler, Randy	T	6-5	255	23	2	Tarleton State
1	Yepremian, Garo	K	5-8	165	24	3	None
85	Zawadzkas, Jerry	TE	6-4	225	21	2	Columbia

DETROIT LIONS   1968 Top Rookies

NAME	POS.	HT.	WT.	AGE	COLLEGE	HOW ACQUIRED*
DePoyster, Jerry	P-FG	6-1	199	22	Wyoming	D-2
Eddy, Nick	RB	6-1	205	23	Notre Dame	D-2, '66
Landry, Greg	QB	6-4	205	21	Massachusetts	D-1a
McCullough, Earl	FL	5-11	172	22	Southern California	D-1b
Mooney, Ed	LB	6-2	238	23	Texas Tech	D-4
Odle, Phil	WE	5-11	187	25	Brigham Young	D-5
Sanders, Charles	TE	6-4	215	22	Minnesota	D-3

*D — Draft (Number indicates draft round)
FA — Free Agent

DETROIT LIONS   1968 Schedule

Sept. 15 — at Dallas	1:30	Nov. 3 — at Los Angeles	1:00
Sept. 22 — Chicago	1:15	Nov. 10 — Baltimore	1:15
Sept. 29 — at Green Bay	1:00	Nov. 17 — at Minnesota	3:00
Oct. 6 — Minnesota	1:15	Nov. 24 — New Orleans	1:15
Oct. 13 — at Chicago	1:00	Nov. 28 — Philadelphia	12:15
Oct. 20 — Green Bay	1:15	Dec. 8 — at Atlanta	1:15
Oct. 27 — San Francisco	1:15	Dec. 15 — at Washington	1:15

GREEN BAY PACKERS

If the opposition, or for that matter pro football fans, are expecting the Packers to be less of a ball club because of the retirement of coach Vince Lombardi, I personally feel they're making a big mistake.

Taking nothing away from Lombardi, Phil Bengston has been far more responsible for the Packers' success than is generally realized. He has been in almost complete control of the Packers' defense since Lombardi brought his "magic" to Green Bay in 1959, and, as I said earlier, it's defense that wins, not offense. Bengston, like Lombardi, is a proponent of simple football played to the hilt. He'll demand the same dedication and discipline that was the Lombardi trademark, and from talking with friends of mine on the Packers, you can bet he'll get it.

The Packers are winners. They've been "there" and while they have aged somewhat, they have, through the organizational skill of Lombardi (who remains on in this capacity), carefully acquired the necessary youth to fill in where it is most needed.

Francis Peay, acquired from the Giants in a two-for-one trade, should be the perfect backup man for tackles Forrest Gregg and Bob Skoronski. Travis Williams, an unknown a year ago, should step into a starter's role in this, his second year, and with the kind of coaching he receives at Green Bay, he has the potential to become another Gale Sayers.

Still, it's quarterback Bart Starr who is the heart of the Packers. A 12-year veteran, Starr, the Phi Beta Kappa out of Alabama in 1955, has completed 58 percent of everything he has thrown since breaking in in 1956. Last year, even though bothered by injuries, he led the Packers to the NFL title and their second consecutive Super Bowl win.

Starr brings the Packers' offense to life. He probes with, and establishes, the running game, while selecting his passes like a skilled surgeon. He seldom gambles (he seldom has to), but he most certainly will when the situation is right. It's hard to say what Starr's favorite pass might be. He can throw both long and short, but he has had remarkable success with the turn-in to any one of his three receivers. This is the turn-in to his tight end, Marv Fleming, a pass that can be looked for on a third and long yardage (six to twelve yards).

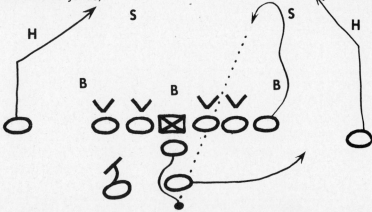

Another pass that Starr likes, and he'll use this on short-yardage plays, is a fake to the fullback — off-tackle — with the halfback running a fly pattern to the outside. This pass is extremely effective because the Packers have a high frequency of using this running play, with the same line action, in similar short-yardage situations.

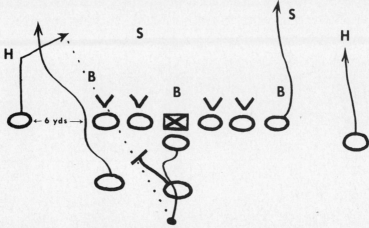

The Packers' running game, while still suffering from the "ghosts" of Jimmy Taylor and Paul Hornung, this year should stand on its own two feet.

The reasons . . . Jim Grabowski, Donny Anderson, and Travis Williams. Grabowski, coming off knee surgery, could become another Jimmy Taylor. They are almost look-alikes in physique, and Grabowski has already indicated he can run the slant off-tackle and the quick trap up the middle — the two plays that made Taylor a great threat.

It's difficult to pick out a key man in the Packers' offensive line. At times they look more like a single unit than six individuals. With Fred Thurston and Jerry Kramer at the guards, Ken Bowman at center, Forrest Gregg and Bob Skoronski at tackles, and Marv Fleming at the tight end, there is little the Packers can't do offensively.

Perhaps what they do best is the power sweep, a play designed originally by Lombardi in 1954 and attempted by almost every team since. The key block here is by the tight end. He must get a stalemate with the strong-

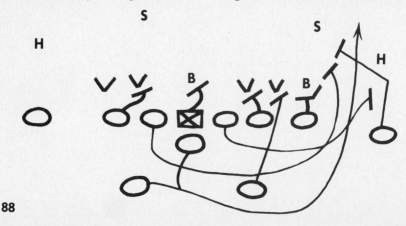

side linebacker, allowing both guards to clear the end. What Lombardi wants on this play is a seal to the inside and outside with an open alley for the running back to turn upfield.

The Packers on defense, like their offensive teammates, are not fancy. They play, number one, to beat you, and number two, to make you beat yourself. You'll seldom find a Packer defensive man out of position, and never out of position twice. They are basically a four-three defensive team, but will show the odd-man Frisco fronts.

Willie Davis and Lionel Aldridge are the prime pass rushers, and their three linebackers — Ray Nitschke, Dave Robinson, and Lee Roy Caffee — are strong against both run and pass.

In the secondary, the man who makes a habit of breaking up ball games is Willie Wood, the right safety. Willie has a sixth sense (and a lot of football sense) about where the ball is going to be thrown. He is not a free safety because, as mentioned before, the Packers do not switch safeties. But since most teams send their flankers to the right, he often is free to roam the secondary, helping the other deep men, Herb Adderley, Bob Jeter, and Tom Brown.

The Packers' red-dog frequency is not high. They like the weak-side linebacker in the dog and occasionally will send both the weak-side linebacker and the middle linebacker. Their most frequent dog down is second and long.

GREEN BAY PACKERS   1968 Veterans Roster

NO.	NAME	POS.	HT.	WT.	AGE	YRS. IN NFL	COLLEGE
26	Adderley, Herb	DB	6-0	200	29	8	Michigan State
82	Aldridge, Lionel	DE	6-4	245	27	6	Utah State
44	Anderson, Donny	HB	6-3	210	25	3	Texas Tech
57	Bowman, Ken	C	6-3	230	25	5	Wisconsin
12	Bratkowski, Zeke	QB	6-3	210	36	13	Georgia
78	Brown, Bob	DE	6-5	260	27	3	Arkansas AM&N
40	Brown, Tom	DB	6-1	195	27	5	Maryland
60	Caffey, Lee Roy	LB	6-3	250	27	6	Texas A&M
88	Capp, Dick	TE-LB	6-3	235	24	2	Boston College
34	Chandler, Don	K	6-2	210	34	13	Florida
84	Dale, Carroll	E	6-2	200	30	9	VPI
87	Davis, Willie	DE	6-3	245	34	11	Grambling
86	Dowler, Boyd	E	6-5	225	31	10	Colorado
55	Flanigan, Jim	LB	6-3	240	22	2	Pittsburgh
81	Fleming, Marv	TE	6-4	235	26	6	Utah
68	Gillingham, Gale	G	6-3	255	24	3	Minnesota
33	Grabowski, Jim	FB	6-2	220	24	3	Illinois
75	Gregg, Forrest	T	6-4	250	34	12	SMU
43	Hart, Doug	DB	6-0	190	29	5	Arlington State
13	Horn, Don	QB	6-2	195	23	2	San Diego State
50	Hyland, Bob	C-G	6-5	250	22	2	Boston College
27	James, Claudis	FL	6-2	190	22	2	Jackson State
21	Jeter, Bob	DB	6-1	205	31	6	Iowa
74	Jordan, Henry	DT	6-3	250	33	12	Virginia
77	Kostelnik, Ron	DT	6-4	260	28	8	Cincinnati
64	Kramer, Jerry	G	6-3	245	32	11	Idaho
80	Long, Bob	FL	6-3	205	25	5	Wichita

NO.	NAME	POS.	HT.	WT.	AGE	YRS. IN NFL	COLLEGE
30	Mercein, Chuck	FB	6-2	220	25	4	Yale
66	Nitschke, Ray	LB	6-3	235	31	11	Illinois
71	Peay, Francis	OT	6-5	250	24	3	Missouri
22	Pitts, Elijah	HB	6-1	205	29	8	Philander Smith
89	Robinson, Dave	LB	6-3	240	27	6	Penn State
45	Rowser, John	DB	6-1	180	23	2	Michigan
76	Skoronski, Bob	T	6-3	245	34	11	Indiana
15	Starr, Bart	QB	6-1	190	34	13	Alabama
37	Vandersea, Phil	TE-LB	6-3	235	25	3	Massachusetts
73	Weatherwax, Jim	DL	6-7	260	25	3	Los Angeles State
23	Williams, Travis	HB	6-1	210	22	2	Arizona State
36	Wilson, Ben	FB	6-1	230	28	5	Southern California
24	Wood, Willie	DB	5-10	190	31	9	Southern California

GREEN BAY PACKERS   1968 Top Rookies

NAME	POS.	HT.	WT.	AGE	COLLEGE	HOW ACQUIRED*
Apisa, Bob	F B	6-2	222	22	Michigan State	D-9
Carr, Fred	L B-TE	6-5	238	22	Texas	D-1
Himes, Dick	O T	6-4	244	22	Ohio State	D-1
Lueck, Bill	O G	6-3	235	22	Arizona	D-1
Robinson, John	F L	6-2	196	22	Tennessee A&I	D-4
Stevens, Bill	Q B	6-3	195	23	Texas	D-3

*D — Draft (Number indicates draft round)
FA — Free Agent

GREEN BAY PACKERS   1968 Schedule

Sept. 15 — Philadelphia	1:00		Nov. 3 — Chicago	1:00
Sept. 22 — Minnesota (Milwaukee)	1:00		Nov. 10 — at Minnesota	1:30
Sept. 29 — Detroit	1:00		Nov. 17 — New Orleans (Milwaukee)	1:00
Oct. 6 — at Atlanta	1:30		Nov. 24 — at Washington	1:15
Oct. 13 — Los Angeles (Milwaukee)	1:00		Dec. 1 — at San Francisco	1:00
Oct. 20 — at Detroit	1:15		Dec. 7 — Baltimore	1:00
Oct. 28 — at Dallas	8:30		Dec. 15 — at Chicago	1:00

MINNESOTA VIKINGS

Bud Grant's first year as head coach of an NFL team was concluded last year on notes of disappointment and optimism — disappointment in that his Vikings were able to win only three ball games out of fourteen, and optimism because of the rapid development from midseason on of some of his youthful talent.

1967 was also a year of indoctrination for Grant, who came out of the Canadian football coaching ranks, taking over a team with which he was completely unfamiliar.

His quarterback, Joe Kapp, was also a Canadian transplant, and while he showed occasional brilliance, he was less than consistent. Now Grant has a year of experience, as does Kapp. And the Vikings will also have quarterback Gary Cuozzo, a five-year NFL veteran who showed a great deal of promise two years ago as a Baltimore Colt and again last year with the fledgling New Orleans Saints.

The Vikings' receiving corps has been hurt with the loss of Red Phillips and Marlin McKeever, both starters of a year ago. But the Vikings have added strength in tight end Billy Martin, obtained from Atlanta, and youngsters Bob Grim and Gene Washington, while still lacking experience, are coming along fast and should complement veteran Paul Flatley. Cuozzo, a fine passer, should get more protection from the Viking offensive lines than he had at New Orleans. This line is headed by Grady Alderman, the last of the original Vikings, and Milt Sunde at guard and Mike Tinglehoff at center. Add to that Ron Yary of USC, the Vikings' first-round draft pick, and Cuozzo, not known as a runner, should have the time he needs to pass to receivers who open up more slowly than veterans.

The Vikings' running game is anchored solidly by fullback Bill Brown and by Dave Osborn, along with second-year man Clint Jones. Brown offers all-around ability in that he can pop the middle or go outside on pitches and sweeps. He's a battler of the first order, and on third and short yardage you can expect him to get the call. Osborn and Jones are the men in the Vikings' outside attack. Jones is still feeling his way, but the big speedster has already shown signs of future greatness.

Because of the multiple talents of the Vikings' set backs, Brown, Osborn, and Jones, the Vikings are a team which can concentrate on the "play pass," the pass off a fake of the running play.

Brown is an exceptional receiver, and runs the following pattern as well

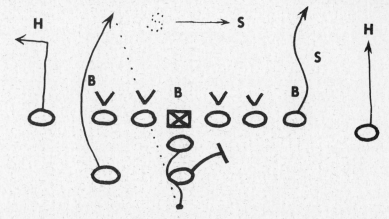

as any back in the league. The above play is called when the Vikings discover that the opposition's defense is attempting to cover fullback Brown with the weak-side linebacker, while double-covering on the flank side.

The best way to stop this pass is to bring the weak-side safety back to play Brown man for man, but then the defense is back on a one-and-one proposition to the flanker side, where Flatley and Washington can work their individual pass cuts.

Flatley runs the following pattern as well as any receiver.

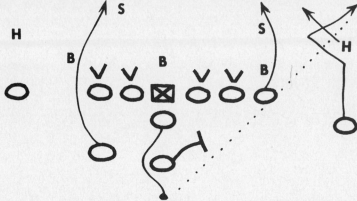

Another pass the Vikings are proficient with is the option pass by Brown.

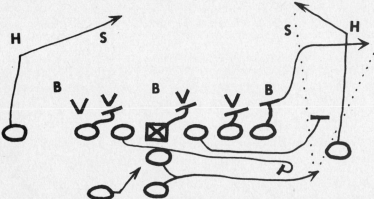

Brown's key is the defensive corner man. If he comes up to stop the run, he can loft the ball either to his long receiver or the tight end coming across into the defensive halfback's vacated area.

On crucial third and long yardage, look for this pass over the middle to tight end Billy Martin.

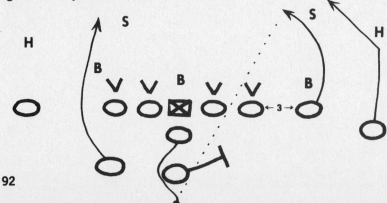

On defense, the Vikings present a very capable front. Defensive end Jim Marshall is one of the finest in the league. He is the one the Vikings call on for a strong pass rush, and he has the size and speed to produce. His best rush is from the outside, and he is so quick that he can often take a circuitous route around the blocking tackle and still reach the quarterback before he can release the ball.

Carl Eller is another speedy defensive end who has the size and strength to work at the tackle spot when and if Grant can find a suitable replacement at the end position.

The linebacking corps is maybe the club's biggest asset. Lonnie Warwick has the natural ability that the middle spot demands, and he has now gained the experience that is necessary there. His biggest plus is quickness into the tackle holes against running plays, and this secondary defense allows linemen Marshall and Eller a little more freedom on their pass-rush routes.

Outside linebackers Roy Winston and John Kirby are also quick and, working with the speedy front four of the Vikings, apply great pressure on quarterbacks with the red-dog.

In the secondary, the Vikings are able subscribers to the zone defense. Ed Sharockman, Earsell Mackbee, Karl Kassulke, and Dale Hackbart are all good operatives of the zone and prefer this defense on first and ten, and on the sure pass situations that occur with third and long.

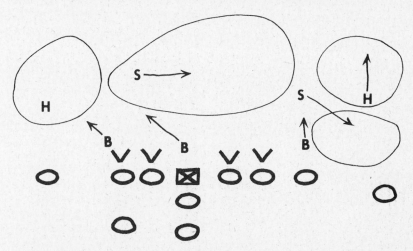

In summation, the Vikings are a team that can run the ball well to the outside with Osborn, but offer a much stronger passing threat, principally with play-fake action. Brown is a dangerous receiver coming out of the backfield. Flatley is tops at working crossing patterns at medium depth.

On defense, passers will see a lot of zone, some dogging from the corner linebackers, and strong pressure from Carl Eller and Jim Marshall.

MINNESOTA VIKINGS   1968 Veterans Roster

NO.	NAME	POS.	HT.	WT.	AGE	YRS. IN NFL	COLLEGE
67	Alderman, Grady	T	6-2	242	30	9	Detroit
87	Beasley, John	TE	6-3	228	23	2	California
17	Berry, Bob	QB	5-11	190	25	4	Oregon
61	Bowie, Larry	G	6-3	255	28	7	Purdue
75	Breitenstein, B.	T	6-4	270	25	2	Tulsa
30	Brown, Bill	RB	5-11	230	30	9	Illinois
44	Coleman, Al	DB	6-0	190	23	2	Tennessee A&I
14	Cox, Fred	K	5-10	200	29	6	Pittsburgh
15	Cuozzo, Gary	QB	6-1	195	27	6	Virginia
71	Davis, Doug	T	6-4	255	24	3	Kentucky
28	Denny, Earl	RB	6-1	200	23	2	Missouri
76	Dickson, Paul	DT	6-5	250	31	10	Baylor
81	Eller, Carl	DE	6-6	265	26	5	Minnesota
52	Faust, Paul	LB	6-0	221	25	2	Minnesota
85	Flatley, Paul	WE	6-1	187	27	6	Northwestern
19	Fleming, Willie	FL	5-9	180	29	1	Iowa
27	Grim, Bob	FL	6-0	196	23	2	Oregon State
49	Hackbart, Dale	DB	6-4	215	29	7	Wisconsin
86	Hall, Tom	FL	6-1½	195	28	7	Minnesota
55	Hansen, Don	LB	6-3	228	24	3	Illinois
50	Hargrove, Jim	LB	6-2½	233	23	2	Howard Payne
26	Jones, Clinton	RB	6-0	206	23	2	Michigan State
22	Jordan, Jeff	DB	6-3	185	25	4	Tulsa
11	Kapp, Joe	QB	6-3	215	30	2*	California
29	Kassulke, Karl	DB	6-0	195	27	6	Drake
24	Keys, Brady	DB	6-0	185	31	8	Colorado State
36	Kirby, John	LB	6-3	235	26	5	Nebraska
—	Krause, Paul	DB	6-3	195	26	4	Iowa State
77	Larsen, Gary	DT	6-5	255	28	5	Concordia
21	Lindsey, Jim	RB	6-2	210	24	3	Arkansas
46	Mackbee, Earsell	DB	6-1	195	27	4	Utah State
70	Marshall, Jim	DE	6-3	248	30	9	Ohio State
89	Martin, Billy	TE	6-4½	235	25	5	Georgia Tech
41	Osborn, Dave	RB	6-0	203	25	4	North Dakota
88	Page, Alan	DT	6-4	278	23	2	Notre Dame
66	Pentecost, John	G	6-2	250	25	2	UCLA
45	Sharockman, Ed	DB	6-0	200	29	7	Pittsburgh
69	Simkus, Arnold	DE	6-4	245	25	2	Michigan
64	Sunde, Milt	G	6-2	250	25	4	Minnesota
33	Tatman, Pete	RB	6-1	215	23	2	Nebraska
53	Tingelhoff, Mick	C	6-2	237	28	7	Nebraska
51	Tobey, Dave	LB	6-3	233	24	2	Oregon
63	Vellone, Jim	G	6-3	255	24	3	Southern California
39	Walden, Bobby	K	6-0	190	30	5	Georgia
59	Warwick, Lonnie	LB	6-3	246	26	4	Tennessee Tech
84	Washington, Gene	WE	6-3	218	23	2	Michigan State
60	Winston, Roy	LB	5-11	231	28	7	Louisiana State

*Joe Kapp is only a two-year NFL veteran but played eight years with Vancouver, B.C., and Calgary, Alberta, in the Canadian League before joining the Vikings.

MINNESOTA VIKINGS 1968 Top Rookies

NAME	POS.	HT.	WT.	AGE	COLLEGE	HOW ACQUIRED*
Freeman, Mike	D B	5-11	169	23	Fresno State	D-4
Goodridge, Bob	WE-DB	6-2	202	22	Vanderbilt	D-6
McGill, Mike	L B	6-2	237	22	Notre Dame	D-3
Reed, Oscar	R B	5-11	221	22	Colorado State	D-7
Sakal, Tom	D B	6-1	193	21	Minnesota	D-10
Yary, Ron	T	6-6	265	22	Southern California	D-1

*D — Draft (Number indicates draft round)
FA — Free Agent

MINNESOTA VIKINGS 1968 Schedule

Sept. 14 — Atlanta	8:00	Nov. 3 — Washington	1:30
Sept. 22 — Green Bay (Milwaukee)	1:00	Nov. 10 — Green Bay	1:30
Sept. 29 — Chicago	1:30	Nov. 17 — Detroit	3:00
Oct. 6 — at Detroit	1:15	Nov. 24 — at Baltimore	2:00
Oct. 13 — at New Orleans	1:30	Dec. 1 — Los Angeles	1:30
Oct. 20 — Dallas	1:30	Dec. 8 — at San Francisco	1:00
Oct. 27 — at Chicago	1:00	Dec. 15 — at Philadelphia	1:15

ATLANTA FALCONS

The Atlanta Falcons, formed before the start of the 1966 season, have gone the way of youth, and it has paid off, even though the number of victories was less last year than in '66.

Head coach Norb Hecker brought a lot of Vince Lombardi's philosophy to Atlanta from Green Bay, where he served as an assistant coach. Norb says, "Regardless of what is said, it all boils down to winning. That is my philosophy — to win. I concentrate on three things: conditioning, desire, and execution. It's easy to be ordinary, but it takes courage to excel, and we must excel."

In talking with many of the Falcons who have gone through Hecker's training camps, it might be concluded that Hecker was concentrating on one word of that philosophy — execution — and that those being "executed" were the players.

However, the reasoning behind the tough training camps of 1966 and 1967 is fairly obvious. Atlanta, as an expansion team, needed personnel, and the best way to evaluate football players is through the "combat" of training camp. Even though Hecker will not hide behind the injury excuse, Atlanta's poor record of last year must in part be a result of several early-season crippling injuries. Both starting guards were lost, and quarterback

Randy Johnson worked the major part of the season with a severe abdominal muscle pull.

Now once again healthy, Johnson, pushed by veterans Terry Nofsinger and Ron VanderKelen, should have his best year. In charge of an offense that greatly resembles that of the Green Bay Packers, Randy uses set backs Perry Lee Dunn and Junior Coffee very effectively, while displaying an arm that promises a big future. Like the Packers, the Falcons use the weak-side slant as a key running play in short-yardage situations. Junior Coffee has

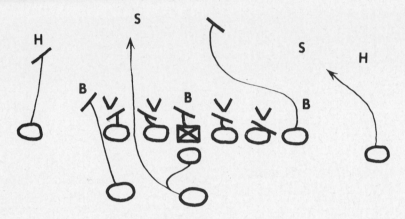

the size for this play and, though not extremely fast, he is big, shifty, and hard to bring down.

He is also a good power-sweep man and, primarily through the slant and sweep, racked up 722 yards in 1967.

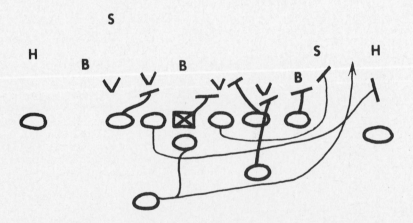

Randy Johnson's receivers, while lacking a great deal of speed, have some nifty moves, and last year's midseason acquisition of Ray Ogden and Jerry Simmons has added strength to that department. One pass pattern at which Johnson became proficient was the two-back circle pass. On this pass,

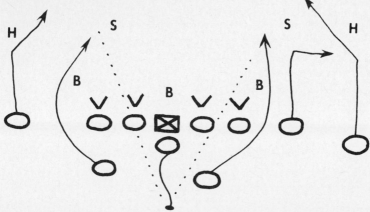

used a great deal on third-and-"must" situations, both backs circle around the defensive ends, and Johnson keys the middle linebacker and hits the back he does not cover. It was successful for the Falcons because both Dunn and Junior Coffee are fine receivers and had experience with this pass before coming to Atlanta — Dunn with Dallas and Coffee with Green Bay.

On defense, the Falcons are again similar to Green Bay, in appearance if not in effect. At the middle-linebacker spot is Tommy Nobis, destined to become one of the game's greatest. Nobis, now in his third year, has been helped by the Falcons' staying away from any great frequency of complicated red-dogging, which has allowed this young man to concentrate on the chores of middle linebacking in the straight four-three defense.

Another advantage of this defensive approach is that it allows Nobis and veteran linebackers Marion Rushing and Ralph Heck to help the defensive secondary. Lee Calland and Ken Reeves are the strong points of the Falcon's four-deep setup that generally will be in a man-to-man key, with the free safety helping out against the offensive strength.

ATLANTA FALCONS   1968 Veterans Roster

NO.	NAME	POS.	HT.	WT.	AGE	YRS. IN NFL	COLLEGE
57	Absher, Dick	LB	6-4	250	23	2	Maryland
80	Barnes, Gary	E-FL	6-4	210	29	6	Clemson
48	Bleick, Tom	DB	6-2½	200	25	3	Georgia Tech
51	Bowling, Andy	LB	6-2	235	22	2	VPI
22	Calland, Lee	DB	6-0	190	27	6	Louisville
34	Coffey, Junior	RB	6-1	210	26	4	Washington
37	Dunn, Perry Lee	RB	6-2	215	27	5	Mississippi
25	Fitzgerald, Mike	DB	5-10	180	27	3	Iowa State
67	Grimm, Dan	G	6-3	245	27	6	Colorado
64	Harmon, Tom	T	6-4	238	23	2	Gustavus Adolphus
55	Heck, Ralph	LB	6-1	230	26	6	Colorado
49	Hudlow, Floyd	DB	5-11	195	24	1	Arizona
11	Johnson, Randy	QB	6-3	196	24	3	Texas A&I
73	Linden, Errol	T	6-5	250	30	8	Houston
26	Lothridge, Billy	K	6-1	190	26	5	Georgia Tech
8	McDonald, Tommy	FL	5-9	175	34	12	Oklahoma
33	Mankins, Jim	RB	6-1	235	24	2	Florida State
53	Marchlewski, Frank	C	6-2	240	24	4	Minnesota

NO.	NAME	POS.	HT.	WT.	AGE	YRS. IN NFL	COLLEGE
21	Moore, Tom	RB	6-2	215	30	9	Vanderbilt
60	Nobis, Tommy	LB	6-2	235	24	3	Texas
14	Nofsinger, Terry	QB	6-4	215	30	8	Utah
70	Norton, Jim	DT	6-4	254	25	4	Washington
28	Ogden, Ray	TE	6-5	225	25	4	Alabama
83	Pope, Bucky	SE	6-5	195	27	4	Catawba
27	Rassas, Nick	DB	6-0	190	24	3	Notre Dame
36	Reaves, Ken	DB	6-3	205	23	3	Norfolk State
29	Rector, Ron	RB	6-0	200	24	3	Northwestern
68	Richards, Bobby	DE	6-2	245	29	7	LSU
43	Richardson, Jerry	DB	6-3	190	26	5	West Texas State
20	Riggle, Bob	DB	6-1	200	24	3	Penn State
74	Rubke, Karl	DT	6-4	244	32	12	Southern California
52	Rushing, Marion	LB	6-2½	230	32	8	Southern Illinois
61	Sandeman, Bill	T	6-6	249	25	3	Pacific
78	Shay, Jerry	DT	6-3	245	24	3	Purdue
77	Sieminski, Chuck	DT	6-5	270	28	6	Penn State
44	Simmons, Jerry	E	6-1	189	25	4	Bethune-Cookman
66	Simon, Jim	G-T	6-4	240	28	6	Miami (Fla.)
71	Szczecko, Joe	DT	6-0	245	26	3	Northwestern
72	Talbert, Don	T	6-5	255	28	5	Texas
7	Traynhan, Wade	K	6-2	218	26	3	Frederick
15	VanderKelen, Ron	QB	6-1	195	28	6	Wisconsin
88	Williams, Sam	DE	6-5	245	37	10	Michigan State
81	Wood, Bo	C	6-3	225	22	2	North Carolina

ATLANTA FALCONS   1968 Top Rookies

NAME	POS.	HT.	WT.	AGE	COLLEGE	HOW ACQUIRED*
Carroll, Leo	DB	6-7	250	24	San Diego State	Trade
Dabney, Carlton	DE-DT	6-4½	250	21	Morgan State	D-2
Eber, Rick	FL	6-0	173	21	Tulsa	D-6 (Balt.)
Hagle, Jim	RB	6-2	200	21	SMU	D-6
Humphrey, Claude	DE	6-5	255	23	Tennessee State	D-1
Wright, John	FL	6-0	195	22	Illinois	D-2 (L.A.)
Wynns, Joe	DB	6-1	192	22	S. Carolina State	D-6 (Pittsburgh)

*D — Draft (Number indicates draft round)
FA — Free Agent

ATLANTA FALCONS   1968 Schedule

Sept. 14 — at Minnesota	8:00	Nov. 3 — Pittsburgh	1:15
Sept. 22 — Baltimore	1:30	Nov. 10 — Los Angeles	1:15
Sept. 29 — at San Francisco	1:00	Nov. 17 — at Chicago	1:00
Oct. 6 — Green Bay	1:30	Nov. 24 — at St. Louis	1:00
Oct. 13 — New York	1:30	Dec. 1 — at Baltimore	2:00
Oct. 20 — at Los Angeles	1:00	Dec. 8 — Detroit	1:15
Oct. 27 — at Cleveland	1:30	Dec. 15 — San Francisco	1:15

BALTIMORE COLTS

While Baltimore is known primarily as a passing team under the guidance of Johnny Unitas, head coach Don Shula says, "We like to keep as close a balance as possible between running and passing so that we can keep the defenses guessing. Defensively, we want to stop the long run and the long pass, the easy touchdown. We feel if we make the other team's offense grind it out, sooner or later they're going to make a mistake."

Shula puts his philosophy into practice. In 1967, the Colts attempted 457 passes and ran the ball 443 times, which is almost a 50-50 split.

On the ground, the Colts use set backs Tony Lorick and Tom Matte for the bulk of their running game, which is mainly inside and features the draw play, as with most good passing teams. The Colts use several variations of the draw, and like all draw plays they are designed not only to break the running back into the open but to keep the defensive pass rush honest. Against the draw, defensive linemen must play it honest. If they leave

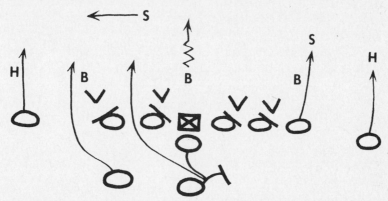

their assigned pass-rush routes in wild attempts to get to the quarterback, they are going to be beaten by the draw. This effect of the draw for a passing team like Baltimore is almost as important as the yardage gained from the play. It helps the offensive line give quarterback Johnny Unitas that extra split second to coordinate with receivers like Ray Perkins, Willie Richardson, and John Mackey. When you watch the Colts, look for many draws and plenty of passing.

Johnny Unitas is as cool a quarterback as ever came down the pike. He has been labeled a burglar because he appears to gamble more than other top quarterbacks. However, many times what appears to be a gamble is not that to Unitas. He has extreme confidence in his own ability and that of his receivers. He can throw both long and short as well as any quarterback ever has, and the men he works best with are his receivers, Ray Perkins at end and Willie Richardson at flanker. This is one of John's favorite third-down passes. Unitas, Perkins, and Richardson have timed it to the point where they could probably complete it blindfolded. Perkins or Richardson

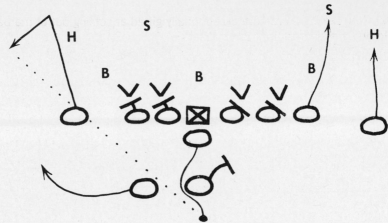

drives off the line of scrimmage to the outside shoulder of the man who is attempting to cover him. He then drives hard downfield, making the defender move with him. When he gets the defender moving back, he plants his inside foot and breaks sharply to the sideline, with a slight angle back toward the line of scrimmage. This is a pass Baltimore will use on third and long yardage (four to twelve yards) or near the half or end of a game, when the receiver, following the completion, can step out of bounds and kill the clock.

This is Baltimore's sideline-and-up move. The receiver drives to the half-

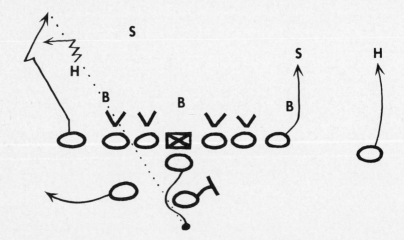

back, fakes to the sideline, and then, as the defender comes back to cover the move to the sideline, he will break straight downfield. The Colts will usually use this after completing several sideline passes, or when a defender starts to play too close. It could even be a game opener, with the defense expecting the Colts to go with more of a ball-control attack.

Along with Tom Matte, the off-season acquisition of Timmy Brown from Philadelphia has given Unitas an even stronger passing attack, even though he lost through retirement the game's greatest receiver, Raymond Berry.

Matte and Brown are both exceptionally gifted at coming out of the back-field and working on linebackers that are forced into a man-to-man situation by the need to double-cover the Colts' outside receivers.

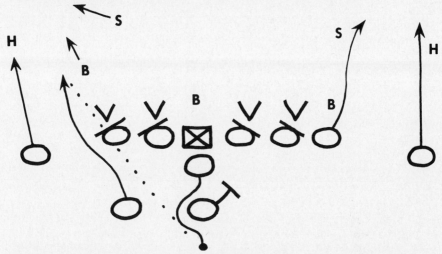

The same pressure by the Colts' outside receivers also enables big John Mackey, the Colts' tight end, to work man-to-man on the opposition's tight

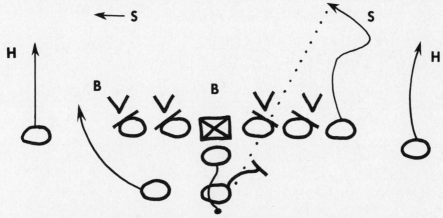

safety. Mackey came up with 55 catches last year for nearly 700 yards, and his blocking skill is one of the big factors that upholds Coach Don Shula's philosophy of splitting the game between the pass and the run.

Defensively, the Colts show several fronts, the four-three and the odd Friscos. They red-dog linebackers in many situations, but prefer a zone on a sure pass situation, with the linebackers dropping back into the pass defense.

They have tremendous speed in their secondary, with Bobby Boyd, the left corner man, the man most adept at the interception. Boyd, not an exceptionally fast man, is very quick and well versed on the receivers he must cover man-to-man. Lenny Lyles, the other corner man, has great speed, and while he is not high on the interception list, it could be because the opposition considers him a man to be avoided.

When watching the Colts' defense, look for the red-dog by one or more linebackers on second and long, and the zone defense on third and long.

BALTIMORE COLTS   1968 Veterans Roster

NO.	NAME	POS.	AGE.	HT.	WT.	YRS. IN NFL	COLLEGE
29	Alley, Don	FL	23	6-3	200	2	Adams State
73	Ball, Sam	T	24	6-4	240	3	Kentucky
40	Boyd, Bob	DB	30	5-10	192	9	Oklahoma
81	Braase, Ordell	DE	36	6-4	245	12	South Dakota
44	Brown, Timmy	RB	31	5-11	198	10	Ball State
48	Carr, Henry	DB	26	6-3	195	4	Arizona State
50	Curry, Bill	LB-C	26	6-2	235	4	Georgia Tech
32	Curtis, Mike	LB	24	6-2	232	4	Duke
63	Davis, Norman	G	23	6-2	245	2	Grambling
53	Gaubatz, Dennis	LB	28	6-2	232	6	LSU
42	Harold, George	DB	26	6-3	194	3	Allen
25	Hawkins, Alex	E-FL	31	6-1	186	10	South Carolina
45	Hill, Jerry	RB	28	5-11	215	7	Wyoming
85	Hilton, Roy	DE	25	6-6	240	4	Jackson State
49	Lee, David	K	24	6-4	215	3	Louisiana Tech
20	Logan, Jerry	DB	27	6-1	190	6	West Texas State
33	Lorick, Tony	RB	27	6-1	217	5	Arizona State
43	Lyles, Lenny	DB	32	6-2	204	11	Louisville
88	Mackey, John	TE	26	6-2	224	6	Syracuse
41	Matte, Tom	RB	29	6-0	214	8	Ohio State
79	Michaels, Lou	DE-K	31	6-2	250	11	Kentucky
76	Miller, Fred	DT	28	6-3	250	6	ISU
28	Orr, Jimmy	FL	32	5-11	185	11	Georgia
26	Pearson, Preston	DB	23	6-1	190	2	Illinois
27	Perkins, Ray	E	26	6-0	183	2	Alabama
55	Porter, Ron	LB	23	6-3	232	2	Idaho
62	Ressler, Glenn	G	25	6-3	250	4	Penn State
87	Richardson, Willie	FL	28	6-2	198	6	Jackson State
66	Shinnick, Don	LB	33	6-0	228	12	UCLA
74	Smith, Billy Ray	DT	33	6-4	250	10	Arkansas
78	Smith Bubba	DE	23	6-7	295	2	Michigan State
47	Stukes, Charles	DB	23	6-3	212	2	Maryland State
83	Stynchula, Andy	DT-DE	29	6-3	250	9	Penn State
71	Sullivan, Dan	G	29	6-3	250	7	Boston College
52	Szymanski, Dick	C	35	6-3	235	13	Notre Dame
19	Unitas, John	QB	35	6-1	196	13	Louisville
72	Vogel, Bob	T	26	6-5	250	6	Ohio State
21	Volk, Rick	DB	23	6-3	195	2	Michigan
16	Ward, Jim	QB	24	6-2	195	2	Gettysburg
46	Welch, Jim	DR	30	6-0	196	9	SMU
86	Wilson, Butch	TE	26	6-2	228	6	Alabama

BALTIMORE COLTS   1968 Top Rookies

NAME	POS.	HT.	WT.	AGE	COLLEGE	HOW ACQUIRED*
Detwiler, Jim	HB	6-3	220	22	Michigan	D-1, '67
Duncan, James	DB	6-2	200	22	Maryland State	D-4
Grant, Bob	LB	6-2	225	21	Wake Forest	D-2

NAME	POS.	HT.	WT.	AGE	COLLEGE	HOW ACQUIRED*
O'Hara, Rich	E	6-3	210	23	Northern Arizona	D-3
Rein, Bo	E	6-0	185	22	Ohio State	D-7, '67
Williams, John	T	6-3	256	22	Minnesota	D-1

*D — Draft (Number indicates draft round)
FA — Free Agent

BALTIMORE COLTS   1968 Schedule

Sept. 15 — San Francisco	2:00	Nov. 3 — at New York	1:30
Sept. 22 — at Atlanta	1:30	Nov. 10 — at Detroit	1:15
Sept. 29 — at Pittsburgh	1:30	Nov. 17 — St. Louis	2:00
Oct. 6 — Chicago	2:00	Nov. 24 — Minnesota	2:00
Oct. 13 — at San Francisco	1:00	Dec. 1 — Atlanta	2:00
Oct. 20 — Cleveland	2:00	Dec. 7 — at Green Bay	1:00
Oct. 27 — Los Angeles	2:00	Dec. 15 — at Los Angeles	1:00

SAN FRANCISCO FORTY-NINERS

The San Francisco Forty-Niners have many questions to answer during the season of 1968. Dick Nolan, a former teammate of mine and more recently the defensive master of the Dallas Cowboys, takes over as head coach from the departed Jack Christiansen.

Make no mistake about it, Nolan is defensively oriented. He believes, like a lot of winning coaches, that it's defense that makes the difference. And while the Forty-Niners haven't been setting the world on fire, they have the personnel to activate Nolan's theories.

One statistic alone is enough to tell you the Forty-Niners' defensive line is capable. While ranking only fifth in overall pass defense, they nevertheless led the NFL in dropping the opposition's quarterback. This line is led by Roland Lakes, Clark Miller, and Charlie Krueger.

The Forty-Niners also get at times some of the best linebacking in the league, from all-pro Dave Wilcox, Matt Hazeltine, and middleman Ed Beard. The secondary, too, is capable and showed poorly last year only because of numerous injuries. Jimmy Johnson, back from an injury, and Kermit Alexander anchor this group, with Johnson one of the best at man-to-man coverage.

While playing many defenses over the past years, this season you can look for the Forty-Niners to stay exclusively with the four-three. It's what Dick Nolan knows and relies upon, and if he's as effective with the Forty-Niners as he's been with Dallas, San Francisco will start turning over the ball to the offense far more regularly than they have in the past.

The Forty-Niners' offensive game will also offer question marks over Nolan's shakedown season. At the all-important quarterback position, George Mira will be making a strong bid to move in ahead of veteran John Brodie. The two are very dissimilar in style of play and this could be a problem if the Forty-Niners continue to try and alternate the two. Brodie is a drop-back passer with, at times, an incredible arm, while Mira is a Fran Tarkenton-type scrambler. The two styles just don't fit into the same offense.

The Forty-Niners have several fine receivers, with split end Dick Witcher the most productive. Witcher has all the moves for both the short game and the long, and exceptional running ability when he comes down with it.

He is at his best against man-to-man coverage, where he specializes in the square-outs at necessary depths.

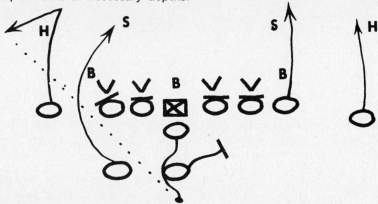

Dave Parks, coming off a 1967 injury, is also a fine receiver and is a good first-down man on the split-end "turn-in," which he runs after faking a fly pattern.

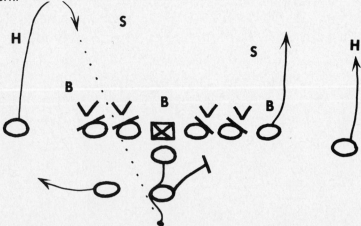

For pure brute strength, the Forty-Niners have another exceptional receiver in Monte Stickles, their big tight end who specializes in blocking but has on many occasions come up with the big first down over the middle.

The Forty-Niners' two set backs are also fine receivers, with John David Crow the best receiver of the Ken Willard-Crow combination. John, a long-time veteran, works extremely well against linebackers, either from the set backfield or from the flanker formation.

His favorite route is one that is used by many teams, but is nevertheless

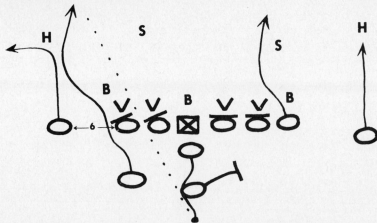

effective because of Crow's exceptional feel. On the above, Crow will drive at the linebacker as if he is going to block for Willard on the off-tackle. As the linebacker comes up to make the tackle, Crow breaks around him and finds the open spot. The Forty-Niners like this play on third and extremely short yardage, when the defense is anticipating Willard's first-down slant.

Another play to watch for with Brodie in the game is the long pass on the third down and medium-long situation, such as third and four. Brodie and Parks are specialists in faking the short square-out, with Parks pulling the defender up and then breaking downfield.

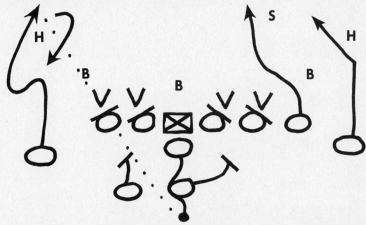

The Forty-Niners' running game is a powerful one, with Ken Willard and John David Crow running behind a seasoned line that includes three all-star performers: center Bruce Bosley and guards John Thomas and Howard Mudd.

This trio concentrates on the quick-opening holes between tackles and the quick trap blocks that are extremely effective for a team like the Forty-Niners that must be given a hard pass rush. The Forty-Niners also use,

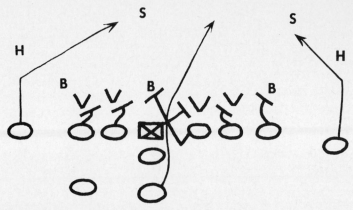

as do all teams that major in the pass game, a number of draw plays. These plays are effective in themselves, but primarily they are used to keep the defensive pass rush honest.

In summation, the Forty-Niners can be expected to improve dramatically on defense and, if the offense can settle down to any kind of consistency, they could become a threat to the Rams and Baltimore in the Coastal Division.

SAN FRANCISCO FORTY-NINERS   1968 Veterans Roster

NO.	NAME	POS.	HT.	WT.	AGE	YRS. IN NFL	COLLEGE
39	Alexander, Kermit	DB	5-11	180	27	6	UCLA
50	Beard, Ed	LB	6-1	226	28	4	Tennessee
77	Bosley, Bruce	C	6-2	244	34	13	West Virginia
12	Brodie, John	QB	6-1	210	33	12	Stanford
56	Cerne, Joe	G	6-2	240	26	4	Northwestern
66	Collett, Elmer	G	6-4	244	23	2	San Francisco State
44	Crow, John David	RB	6-2	224	32	11	Texas A&M
42	Cunningham, Doug	RB	6-0	193	22	2	Mississippi
29	Daugherty, Bob	RB	6-1	210	26	2	Tulsa
36	Davis, Tommy	K	6-0	220	33	10	LSU
20	Donnelly, George	DB	6-3	210	26	4	Illinois
35	Gonsoulin, Austin	DB	6-4	213	30	2	Baylor
54	Harrison, Bob	LB	6-2	228	31	10	Oklahoma
–	Hays, Harold	LB	6-2	225	29	6	Mississippi Southern
55	Hazeltine, Matt	LB	6-1	230	35	14	California
80	Hindman, Stan	DE	6-3	232	24	3	Mississippi
87	Holzer, Tom	DE	6-4	248	23	2	Louisville
38	Jackson, Jim	DB	5-11	193	24	3	Western Illinois
72	Johnson, Charlie	DT	6-1	265	24	3	Louisville
37	Johnson, Jim	DB	6-2	187	30	8	UCLA
58	Johnson, Walt	DE	6-5	235	24	2	Tuskegee
43	Jordan, Jimmy	RB	6-1	200	24	2	Florida
70	Krueger, Charlie	DT	6-4	260	31	10	Texas A&M
60	Lakes, Roland	DT	6-4	279	28	8	Wichita
22	Lewis, Gary	RB	6-2	230	26	5	Arizona State
26	McFarland, Kay	FL	6-2	186	30	6	Colorado State
74	Miller, Clark	DE	6-5	247	30	7	Utah State
10	Mira, George	QB	5-11	190	26	5	Miami (Fla.)
68	Mudd, Howard	G	6-2	254	26	5	Hillsdale (Mich.)
46	Myers, Chip	E	6-4	190	23	2	Northwestern State (Okla.)
57	Nunley, Frank	LB	6-2	230	23	2	Michigan

106

NO.	NAME	POS.	HT.	WT.	AGE	YRS. IN NFL	COLLEGE
84	Olerich, Dave	TE	6-1	220	22	2	San Francisco U.
63	Parker, Don	G	6-3	258	24	2	Virginia
81	Parks, Dave	E	6-2	207	26	5	Texas Tech
32	Phillips, Mel	DB	6-2	192	24	3	N. Carolina A&T
83	Randle, Sonny	E	6-2	190	32	10	Virginia
27	Randolph, Alvin	DB	6-2	192	24	3	Iowa
67	Rock, Walt	T	6-5	255	28	6	Maryland
76	Rohde, Len	T	6-4	250	30	9	Utah State
88	Smith, Steve	DE	6-5	236	24	2	Michigan
11	Spurrier, Steve	QB	6-2	203	23	2	Florida
85	Stickles, Monty	TE	6-4	235	30	9	Notre Dame
78	Thomas, John	G	6-4	250	33	11	Pacific
24	Trimble, Wayne	DB	6-3	203	23	2	Alabama
45	Tucker, Bill	RB	6-2	220	25	2	Tennessee State
64	Wilcox, Dave	LB	6-2	234	25	5	Oregon
40	Willard, Ken	RB	6-2	230	24	4	North Carolina
89	Windsor, Bob	TE	6-4	224	23	2	Kentucky
88	Witcher, Dick	E	6-3	204	24	3	UCLA

SAN FRANCISCO FORTY-NINERS 1968 Top Rookies

NAME	POS.	HT.	WT.	AGE	COLLEGE	HOW ACQUIRED*
Blue, Forrest	C	6-5	248	22	Auburn	D-1
Fuller, John	E	6-0	175	22	Lamar Tech	D-4
Lee, Dwight	R B	6-2	198	21	Michigan State	D-5
Olssen, Lance	O T-DT	6-5	257	20	Purdue	D-3a
Vanderbundt, Skip	L B	6-3	229	21	Oregon State	D-3b

*D— Draft (Number indicates draft round)
FA— Free Agent

SAN FRANCISCO FORTY-NINERS 1968 Schedule

Sept. 15—at Baltimore	2:00	Nov. 3—Cleveland	1:00
Sept. 22—St. Louis	1:00	Nov. 10—at Chicago	1:00
Sept. 29—Atlanta	1:00	Nov. 17—Los Angeles	1:00
Oct. 6—at Los Angeles	1:00	Nov. 24—at Pittsburgh	1:15
Oct. 13—Baltimore	1:00	Dec. 1—Green Bay	1:00
Oct. 20—at New York	1:30	Dec. 8—Minnesota	1:00
Oct. 27—at Detroit	1:15	Dec. 15—at Atlanta	1:15

LOS ANGELES RAMS

The Los Angeles Rams of 1968 have what they call in political circles the "smell" of a winner.

They came close last year, winning their Coastal Division (defeating Baltimore to do so) and only failed to win it all when they lost a crucial play-off game to Green Bay.

The ingredients with which the Rams appear to be headed towards another title are sound and complete. They have the best defensive line in pro football — Dave Jones, Merlin Olsen, Roger Brown, and Lamar Lundy — who terrorized NFL quarterbacks last season. They'll also be bolstered by the return of Roosevelt Grier, who sat out last year with an injured Achilles' tendon. Defensive end Dave Jones is the most feared of this "fearsome foursome" in that not only is he big like all the Rams' defensemen, but he also has uncanny speed and quickness. He is the game's best pass rusher, and Rams' fans often see Jones, working with Merlin Olsen, crush the opposition's quarterback following maneuvers like this.

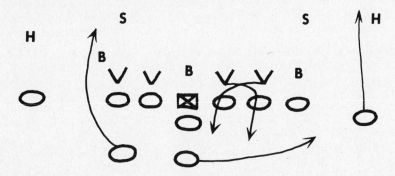

The Rams' linebacking corps is a very effective complement to the Rams' front four. Last year, because of a strong pass rush and heads-up play by outside linebackers Maxie Baughan and Jack Pardee and middle linebacker Doug Woodlief, the Rams led the NFL in interceptions with 32. The Rams are not necessarily a strong red-dogging team in that their front four provides the pass rush while the linebackers drop deep into the secondary, forcing a quarterback to throw over (or over-throw) them.

In the secondary, the Rams have a little bit of everything. Irv Cross at the right corner is a talented and skilled defender, and as good on the man-to-man defense as any defender in the league. He is complemented by Maxie Baughan, the linebacker on his side, with whom he has worked for many years, now as a Ram, and before 1966 with Philadelphia.

At the opposite corner is Clancy Williams, a talented defender who doesn't really know how fast he is. He makes mistakes, but many a receiver who has beaten him only to have a ball intercepted or knocked away will tell you he must be the game's quickest defender.

Eddie Meador at the free safety is wise to the ways of the NFL and reads offensive patterns with the best. He has a habit (an annoying one for quarterbacks) of turning up where he shouldn't be and often it pays off with the interception.

The Rams' offense is Roman Gabriel. "Gabe" really arrived last year, setting a Rams' record for touchdown passes with 25 and directing an offense which, while not fancy, was methodical in capitalizing on ball turn-overs by the defense. Gabriel can throw long or short, and he has the size to stay in the pocket fighting off rushers, releasing the ball accurately at the last split second.

This year, backing up Gabriel, the Rams have obtained veteran Milt Plum from the Detroit Lions. Plum has the ability and the experience to play in the NFL, but as long as Gabriel is healthy, Plum will do most of his work on the phone.

The Rams' receivers, like Gabriel, arrived in 1967. They are headed by Bernie Casey, a soft-spoken, dedicated flanker who can go deep but is most effective working the short routes man-to-man against defenders. Look for the following short square-out on "must" short-yardage situations. On

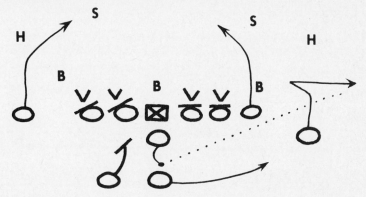

this pattern, Bernie makes the defensive back think he is going to drive to the inside. He then turns back to the outside for the ball, and the necessary first-down yardage. Actually, it is a takeoff on another pattern the Rams and Bernie like, and one that will be called at any time.

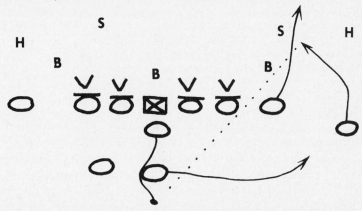

The Rams' running game is built around Les Josephson and Dick Bass. Bass isn't the biggest guy around, but he is difficult to get a hand on. He is exceptional at running the draw play. He seems to have almost a sixth sense as to where the hole is going to open up, and he's built so low to the ground that it is difficult for linemen and linebackers to spot him as the quarterback slips him the ball. Josephson, the Rams' "man for all reasons," is a fine outside runner, and piles up a lot of his yardage on the sweep and the quick pitch to the outside.

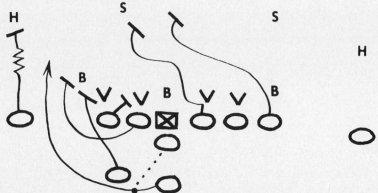

Bass and Josephson are also active in the passing game, and when the Rams are in deep trouble, third and exceptionally long yardage, watch for the screen pass to either.

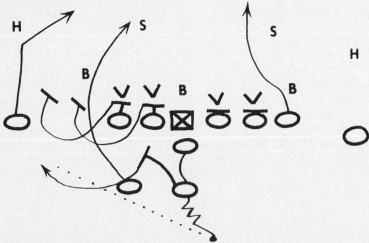

Tommy Mason, recovering from knee surgery, is also a threat in the Rams' running game, capable of running inside as well as outside on power sweeps. Mason is also highly skilled at coming from the set back into pass patterns, and gives Gabriel another valued receiver to work against defensive linebackers.

In summation, the Rams could be headed all the way. They have everything, plus the knowledge gained in 1967 that they indeed can beat the "best."

LOS ANGELES RAMS   1968 Veterans Roster

NO.	NAME	POS.	HT.	WT.	AGE	YRS. IN NFL	COLLEGE
22	Bass, Dick	RB	5-10	195	31	9	Pacific
55	Baughan, Maxie	LB	6-1	230	29	9	Georgia Tech
86	Bedsole, Hal	TE	6-4	235	26	4	Southern California
53	Breen, Gene	LB	6-2	230	27	5	Virginia Tech
78	Brown, Roger	DT	6-5	295	31	9	Maryland State
51	Burman, George	C-G	6-3	255	25	3	Northwestern
70	Cahill, Dave	DT	6-3	245	26	3	Northern Arizona
63	Carollo, Joe	T	6-2	258	28	7	Notre Dame
25	Casey, Bernie	FL	6-4	210	29	8	Bowling Green
62	Chuy, Don	G	6-1	255	27	6	Clemson
73	Cowan, Charlie	T	6-4	265	30	8	New Mexico Highlands
49	Crabb, Claude	DB	6-0	192	28	7	Colorado
27	Cross, Irv	DB	6-1	195	29	8	Northwestern
46	Daniel, Willie	DB	5-11	190	30	8	Mississippi State
35	Dyer, Henry	RB	6-1	230	23	2	Grambling
33	Ellison, Willie	RB	6-1	200	22	2	Texas Southern
18	Gabriel, Roman	QB	6-4	220	28	7	N. Carolina State
30	Gossett, Bruce	PK	6-2	230	26	5	Richmond
76	Grier, Roosevelt	DT	6-5	287	36	12	Penn State
88	Guillory, Anthony	LB	6-4	235	25	3	Lamar Tech
50	Iman, Ken	C	6-1	240	29	8	S.E. Missouri State
75	Jones, Dave	DE	6-5	250	29	8	S. Carolina State
34	Josephson, Les	RB	6-0	207	26	5	Augustana
13	Kilgore, Jon	P	6-1	205	24	4	Auburn
44	Lamson, Chuck	DB	6-0	195	29	7	Wyoming
85	Lundy, Lamar	DE	6-7	250	33	12	Purdue
17	McIlhany, Dan	DB	6-0	190	25	2	Texas A&M
65	Mack, Tom	G	6-3	250	24	3	Michigan
20	Mason, Tommy	RB	6-1	195	29	8	Tulane
21	Meador, Ed	DB	5-11	190	31	10	Arkansas Tech
74	Olsen, Merlin	DT	6-5	270	27	7	Utah State
32	Pardee, Jack	LB	6-2	225	32	11	Texas A&M
83	Pivec, Dave	TE	6-3	230	24	3	Notre Dame
16	Plum, Milt	QB	6-2	205	33	12	Penn State
66	Pottios, Myron	LB	6-2	232	29	8	Notre Dame
58	Sanders, Bob	LB	6-3	235	25	2	North Texas State
81	Schumacher, Gregg	DE	6-2	240	26	2	Illinois
71	Scibelli, Joe	G	6-0	255	29	8	Notre Dame
41	Smith, Ron	DB	6-1	192	25	4	Wisconsin
84	Snow, Jack	E	6-2	190	25	4	Notre Dame
26	Stiger, Jim	RB	5-10	214	28	6	Washington
28	Studstill, Pat	FL-P	6-0	175	30	7	Houston
72	Talbert, Diron	DT	6-5	245	24	2	Texas
87	Truax, Billy	TE	6-5	235	25	5	LSU
14	Tucker, Wendell	E	5-10	185	24	2	S. Carolina State
67	Turner, Herschel	G	6-3½	240	26	4	Kentucky
23	Watkins, Tommy	RB	6-0	195	29	7	Iowa State
24	Williams, Clarence	DB	6-2	194	25	4	Washington State
77	Wilson, Jim	DT	6-3	258	26	4	Georgia
47	Winston, Kelton	DB	6-0	195	27	2	Wiley
57	Woodlief, Doug	LB	6-3	225	24	4	Memphis State

LOS ANGELES RAMS   1968 Top Rookies

NAME	POS.	HT.	WT.	AGE	COLLEGE	HOW ACQUIRED*
Anderson, Billy Guy	Q B	6-1	195	27	Tulsa	D-19, '65F
Jackson, Harold	F L	5-10	175	21	Jackson State	D-12
Jordan, Jeff	R B	6-1	215	23	Washington	FA
LaHood, Mike	G	6-2½	240	23	Wyoming	D-2
Webb, Bobby	C	6-2½	230	21	Southern Mississippi	D-6
Williams, Joe	R B	5-10	172	22	Florida A&M	D-8

*D — Draft (Number indicates draft round)
FA — Free Agent

LOS ANGELES RAMS   1968 Schedule

Sept. 16 — at St. Louis	8:30	Nov. 3 — Detroit	1:00
Sept. 22 — Pittsburgh	1:00	Nov. 10 — at Atlanta	1:15
Sept. 29 — at Cleveland	1:30	Nov. 17 — at San Francisco	1:00
Oct. 6 — San Francisco	1:00	Nov. 24 — New York	1:00
Oct. 13 — Green Bay (Milwaukee)	1:00	Dec. 1 — at Minnesota	1:30
Oct. 20 — Atlanta	1:00	Dec. 8 — Chicago	1:00
Oct. 27 — at Baltimore	2:00	Dec. 15 — Baltimore	1:00

THE AMERICAN FOOTBALL LEAGUE   1968

EASTERN DIVISION

Boston Patriots
Buffalo Bills
Houston Oilers
Miami Dolphins
New York Jets

WESTERN DIVISION

Cincinnati Bengals
Denver Broncos
Kansas City Chiefs
Oakland Raiders
San Diego Chargers

BOSTON PATRIOTS

The Boston Patriots may have finished last in 1967, but if the entire team reflects the thinking of head coach Mike Holovak, they'll be in the Super Bowl this year. Mike is extremely optimistic the Pats can bounce back from last year and his reasoning is basically sound.

He has two of the AFL's genuine super-stars in fullback Jim Nance and linebacker Nick Buoniconti. He also has a solid defensive team headed by an extremely capable front four made up of Bob Dee, Jim Hunt, Houston Antwine, and Larry Eisenhauer, all of whom have been All-League at one time or another.

Rookie Dennis Byrd, the Pats' top pick for 1968, should add strength to that foursome, if indeed he doesn't end up with a starting spot. At the linebacker position, aiding Nick Buoniconti, are Ed Philpott and Doug Satcher. They're not Buonicontis, but they do an adequate job.

In the secondary, the Pats are looking for help from Notre Dame rookie Jim Smithberger. At the corners, John Charles and Leroy Mitchell are both back and they should be much improved over last season when, as rookies, they attracted a lot of the opposition's passing attention.

The Pats are basically a four-three defensive team, and while tough against the run, get hurt by the pass because of their secondary.

On the offense, quarterback Babe Parilli (he can't kid me about his age because we played in the same college All-Star game in 1952) is still the man on the spot. And there's no reason to believe the Babe can't live up to Holovak's many solid votes of confidence. Babe is an exceptional short passer and, regardless of his many years under the center, can still throw the bomb.

Art Graham at split end, Gino Cappelletti at flanker, and Jim Whalen at tight end are Babe's primary targets. Art Graham is the deep man while Cappelletti and Whalen work the underneath patterns. Cappelletti, even though a veteran of nine years in the pro wars, is a terrific third-and-long receiver for Babe, and runs the following zig-out as well as anyone around.

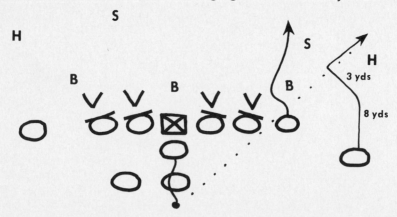

Art Graham is the deep man for the Pats. He was their leading receiver last year with 41 receptions, and he likes the simple patterns such as the fly and the following "over-the-middle pattern," in which Parilli waits until he uncovers the defensive linebackers.

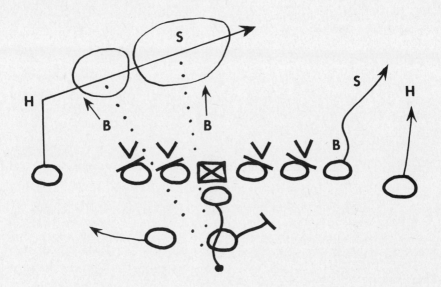

Boston's running game is Jim Nance, and the big fullback gained 1,458 yards last season behind a so-so offensive line. At 6 feet 4 inches and 240 pounds, Nance just bulls for yardage, dragging teammates and tackles along with him. The Patriots like zone blocking for Nance between the tackles, which allows him to find a crack of daylight and make the rest on his own.

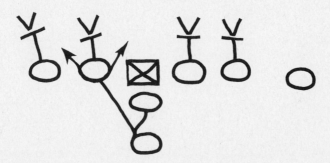

Mike Holovak is hoping that R. C. Gamble will give him the outside threat he needs to make the rushing of Jim Nance even more effective. Should Gamble, a rookie from South Carolina State, make it big, you can look for the following sweep plays.

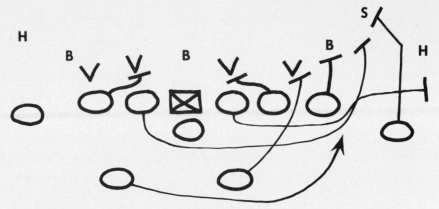

In summation, look for the Patriots to move up the AFL's ladder this year, although they don't appear to be the match of New York or Buffalo.

If they can develop some outside running, Jim Nance may shatter every rushing mark in the book, and he might do it anyway. Babe Parilli should have a good year. He's taken a lot of abuse, but in my book he's still an outstanding quarterback.

BOSTON PATRIOTS   1968 Veterans Roster

NO.	NAME	POS.	HT.	WT.	AGE	YRS. IN PRO	COLLEGE
65	Antwine, Houston	DT	6-0	270	29	8	Southern Illinois
85	Buoniconti, Nick	LB	5-11	220	27	7	Notre Dame
63	Canale, Justin	G	6-2	250	24	4	Mississippi State
33	Cappadona, Bob	HB	6-1	230	25	3	Northeastern
20	Cappelletti, Gino	FLB	6-0	190	34	9	Minnesota
25	Charles, John	DB	6-1	200	23	2	Purdue
81	Colclough, Jim	SpE	6-0	185	31	10	Boston College
21	Cunningham, Jay	DB	5-10	180	25	4	Bowling Green
89	Dee, Bob	DE	6-4	250	32	11	Holy Cross
61	Dudek, Mitch	OT	6-4	250	25	3	Xavier
72	Eisenhauer, Larry	DE	6-5	255	28	8	Boston College
83	Fussell, Tom	DE	6-3	245	22	2	Louisiana State
40	Garron, Larry	HB	6-1	195	31	9	Western Illinois
84	Graham, Art	SpE	6-1	205	27	6	Boston College
79	Hunt, Jim	DT	5-11	255	30	9	Prairie View
45	Ilg, Ray	LB	6-1	220	22	2	Colgate
47	Johnson, Bill	DB	5-10	180	23	3	Nebraska
88	Lamb, Jerry	FL	6-1	190	25	4	Arkansas
24	Leo, Bobby	FLB-HB	5-10	180	23	2	Harvard
76	Long, Charles	G	6-3	250	29	8	Chattanooga
74	Mangum, John	DT	6-1	270	24	3	Southern Mississippi
41	Mitchell, Leroy	DB	6-2	200	23	2	Texas Southern
56	Morris, Jon	C	6-4	240	25	5	Holy Cross
35	Nance, Jim	FB	6-1	240	25	4	Syracuse
77	Neville, Tom	T	6-4	255	24	4	Mississippi State
87	Nichols, Bobby	TE	6-2	220	24	2	Boston U.
71	Oakes, Don	T	6-3	255	29	8	Virginia Tech
15	Parilli, Babe	QB	6-0	190	38	15	Kentucky
52	Philpott, Ed	LB	6-3	240	22	2	Miami (Ohio)
60	St. Jean, Len	G	6-1	240	26	5	Northern Michigan

NO.	NAME	POS.	HT.	WT.	AGE	YRS. IN PRO	COLLEGE
58	Satcher, Doug	LB	6-0	220	24	3	Southern Mississippi
68	Singer, Karl	T	6-3	250	24	3	Purdue
36	Swanson, Terry	K	6-0	210	23	2	Massachusetts
22	Thomas, Gene	HB	6-1	220	25	3	Florida A&M
75	Toner, Ed	DT	6-3	250	24	2	Massachusetts
10	Trull, Don	QB	6-1	190	27	5	Baylor
42	Webb, Don	DB	5-10	200	28	8	Iowa State
82	Whalen, Jim	TE	6-2	210	24	4	Boston College
70	Witt, Mel	DE	6-3	265	22	2	Texas (Arl.)

BOSTON PATRIOTS   1968 Top Rookies

NAME	POS.	HT.	WT.	AGE	COLLEGE	HOW ACQUIRED*
Byrd, Dennis	DE	6-4	260	21	N. Carolina State	D-1
Funches, Tommy	T	6-5	260	21	Jackson State	D-2
Gamble, R. C.	HB	6-3	220	21	S. Carolina State	D-4
Johnson, Daryl	DB	5-11	190	22	Morgan State	D-8
Marsh, Aaron	FI-B	6-1	190	22	Eastern Kentucky	D-3
Smithberger, Jim	DB	6-2	200	21	Notre Dame	D-5

*D — Draft (Number indicates draft round)
FA — Free Agent

BOSTON PATRIOTS   1968 Schedule

Sept. 8 — at Buffalo	2:00	Nov. 3 — Denver	1:30
Sept. 22 — New York (Birmingham)	2:00	Nov. 10 — San Diego	1:30
Sept. 29 — at Denver	2:00	Nov. 17 — at Kansas City	3:00
Oct. 6 — at Oakland	1:00	Nov. 24 — Miami	1:30
Oct. 13 — Houston	1:30	Dec. 1 — Cincinnati	1:30
Oct. 20 — Buffalo	1:30	Dec. 8 — at Miami	1:30
Oct. 27 — at New York	1:30	Dec. 15 — at Houston	3:00

BUFFALO BILLS

The Buffalo Bills, under coach Joe Collier, are a team that could be a serious challenger for an AFL title in 1968. They still have many players who performed on the title teams of 1964 and '65, and barring the incredible injury epidemic that hit them last year they could very well improve on their ten and four record of last year.

Offensively, Jack Kemp is the key to the Bills' scoring ability. Jackie didn't have a top year last year, but there's no reason to suspect he can't return to championship form this year. Kemp is an exciting football player, much in the mold of the Giants' Fran Tarkenton. He can scramble when he has to, but his best game is not a helter-skelter one.

Kemp's production falloff last year could possibly be attributed to problems with receivers. Elbert Dubenion, who in years past has been one of the best around, didn't have his normal year, and because of injuries Kemp's other receivers were constantly undergoing change. This is tough on a quarterback, who needs to see the same "faces" in the huddle the majority of the time.

Along with Dubenion, Kemp's other big outside receiver is Art Powell, who could again become a prime target as a split end, provided that an injured knee comes around.

Last year, however, Kemp's number-one receiver was set back Keith Lincoln. Lincoln can do a lot of things on a football field, and one of them is to get himself open. Running from the halfback position, Lincoln is especially effective when a defensive team is trying to cover him with a linebacker.

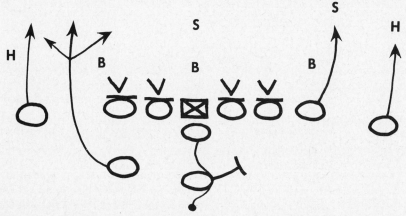

The other set back for the Bills is Wray Carlton. Wray is not a spectacular football player, but is steady and can be counted on week in and week out. His specialty is blocking for Lincoln on sweeps and hitting between tackles on short-yardage situations.

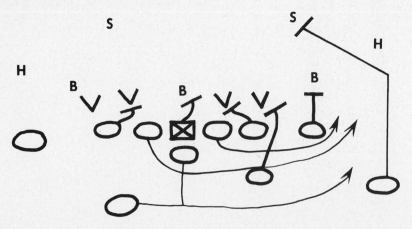

The Bills' defense, like the offense, is not spectacular but basically sound. Right tackle Tom Sestak and left end Ron McDole are the men to watch as pass rushers, while the real strength of the overall units lies with the linebackers. Mike Stratton at right linebacker is as good a red-dogger around, and he teams well with his defensive end in making the moves that get him to the quarterback.

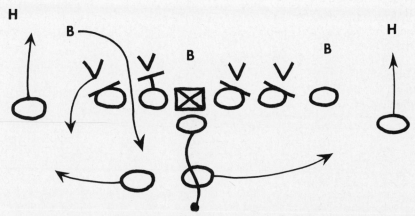

Rounding out the Bills' linebackers are middle linebacker Harry Jacobs and left linebacker Paul Guidry. Jacobs could be the big man for the Bills this year. He had over 70 tackles last year in seven games before injuring a collarbone, and while he isn't the biggest middle man around (224 pounds), his quickness resembles that of a youthful Sam Huff.

The Bills' secondary is a solid unit, with safety men George Saimes and Tom Janik the outstanding performers. Janik had ten interceptions last year, and the two combine to give all AFL quarterbacks a lot of sleepless nights. Both have great speed, which enables them to help out corner backs Butch Byrd and Booker Edgerson.

In summation, the Bills must get a big year out of Jack Kemp. If they are going to win, he will be the one who will pull it off. And they can get that big year if Art Powell can return from knee surgery, Keith Lincoln stays healthy again, and a solid defensive team plays up to its potential.

BUFFALO BILLS 1968 Veterans Roster

NO.	NAME	POS.	HT.	WT.	AGE	YRS. IN PRO	COLLEGE
77	Barber, Stew	T	6-2	252	29	8	Penn State
50	Bemiller, Al	C	6-3	246	29	8	Syracuse
35	Bivins, Charley	HB	6-2	216	29	9	Morris Brown
42	Byrd, George	DB	6-0	208	26	5	Boston U.
30	Carlton, Wray	FB	6-1	224	31	9	Duke
45	Clarke, Hagood	DB	6-0	195	26	5	Florida
82	Costa, Paul	E	6-4	246	26	4	Notre Dame
83	Crockett, Bobby	E	6-2	200	25	2	Arkansas
62	Cunningham, Dick	T	6-2	242	23	2	Arkansas
71	DeSutter, Wayne	T	6-4	255	24	2	Western Illinois
44	Dubenion, Elbert	FL	5-11	187	32	9	Bluffton
78	Dunaway, Jim	DT	6-4	281	26	6	Mississippi

NO.	NAME	POS.	HT.	WT.	AGE	YRS. IN PRO	COLLEGE
24	Edgerson, Booker	DB	5-10	183	29	7	Western Illinois
80	Ferguson, Charley	E	6-5	224	28	7	Tennessee State
16	Flores, Tom	QB	6-1	202	30	8	Pacific
59	Guidry, Paul	LB	6-2	234	24	3	McNeese State
79	Hudson, Dick	T	6-4	262	28	7	Memphis State
64	Jacobs, Harry	LB	6-1	224	31	7	Bradley
27	Janik, Tom	DB	6-3	190	27	6	Texas A&I
65	Jeter, Gene	LB	6-3	235	26	4	Arkansas AM&N
15	Kemp, Jack	QB	6-0	204	33	12	Occidental
73	Kindig, Howard	DE	6-6	255	27	4	Los Angeles State
46	King, Tony	FL	6-1	194	24	2	Findlay
43	Ledbetter, Monte	FL	6-2	185	25	2	N.W. Louisiana State
60	LeMoine, Jim	LB	6-2	245	23	2	Utah State
20	Lincoln, Keith	HB	6-1	216	29	8	Washington State
72	McDole, Ron	DE	6-3	270	28	8	Nebraska
55	Maguire, Paul	LB	6-0	230	30	9	Citadel
87	Masters, Billy*	E	6-5	235	24	2	LSU
7	Mercer, Mike	K	6-0	217	32	8	Arizona State
75	Meredith, Dudley	DT	6-4	290	33	6	Lamar Tech
67	O'Donnell, Joe	G	6-2	252	27	5	Michigan
48	Pitts, John	DB	6-4	218	23	2	Arizona State
84	Powell, Art	E	6-2	214	31	12	San Jose State
40	Rutkowski, Ed	FL	6-0	198	27	6	Notre Dame
26	Saimes, George	DB	5-10	188	26	6	Michigan State
56	Schottenheimer, Marty	LB	6-3	224	24	4	Pittsburgh
70	Sestak, Tom	DT	6-4	260	32	7	McNeese State
66	Shaw, Billy	G	6-2	258	29	8	Georgia Tech
32	Spikes, Jack	FB	6-2	220	29	9	TCU
58	Stratton, Mike	LB	6-3	244	27	7	Tennessee
51	Tracey, John	LB	6-3	228	35	10	Texas A&M

*In Military Service.

BUFFALO BILLS 1968 Top Rookies

NAME	POS.	HT.	WT.	AGE	COLLEGE	HOW ACQUIRED*
Chandler, Edgar	G	6-4	225	22	Georgia	D-4
Gregory, Ben	FB	6-0	220	21	Nebraska	D-5a
McBath, Mike	T	6-4	250	22	Penn State	D-5b
Moses, Haven	FL	6-3	200	22	San Diego State	D-1
Tatarek, Bob	DE	6-4	255	22	Miami	D-2
Trapp, Richard	E	6-1	180	21	Florida	D-3

*D — Draft (Number indicates draft round)
FA — Free Agent

BUFFALO BILLS 1968 Schedule

Sept. 8 — Boston	2:00		Oct. 27 — Houston	1:30
Sept. 15 — Oakland	1:30		Nov. 3 — at New York	1:30
Sept. 22 — at Cincinnati	1:30		Nov. 10 — Miami	1:30
Sept. 29 — New York	1:30		Nov. 17 — San Diego	1:30
Oct. 5 — Kansas City	8:00		Nov. 24 — at Denver	2:00
Oct. 13 — at Miami	1:30		Nov. 28 — at Oakland	1:00
Oct. 20 — at Boston	1:30		Dec. 7 — at Houston	3:30

HOUSTON OILERS

Wally Lemm, as head coach of the Houston Oilers, has an approach to the game of football that is both effective and somewhat contradictory. Lemm believes that "football can only be played well when it's fun," and yet he will tell you he "can't stand a good loser."

Last year, the Oilers didn't have many good losers as they pulled off the incredible feat of going from last place in 1966 to an Eastern championship in 1967. Lemm accomplished the turn around by blending the best overall defense in the AFL with a ball-control running game that was also the best in the American League.

The Oilers' offensive line doesn't have to back away from any team in football. Walt Suggs and Ray Hines are the tackles and they're big and tough. All-pro Sonny Bishop is the top guard and Bobby Maples calls the defenses at center. This front five combine with running backs Hoyle Granger at fullback and Woodie Campbell and Sid Blanks at half to give the Oilers the most potent ground game in the league. And that running game was desperately needed, too, as the Oilers had nothing but problems with their passing game, principally because they didn't get number-one quarterback Pete Beathard until after last year's fourth game, and even then the outside receivers never did come up to the balance of the rest of the club.

Beathard, many feel, is on his way to becoming one of the game's outstanding passers and signal callers. He's big at 6 feet 2 inches and 210 pounds, and has that inherent leadership quality that all the great ones, past and present, had. Last year he picked the Oilers up from the moment he joined them from Kansas City. It was his heady play calling that kept the Oilers in contention and later gave them the AFL's Eastern title.

This year the Oilers are on their way to developing a passing attack to go with their proven running game. They have seasoned veterans in Lionel Taylor, Charley Frazier, and Glenn Bass, but they are taking a long look at Ode Burrell, a second-year man, and Richard Stebbins, a 9.1 sprinter who impressed me a great deal in a rookie trial a year ago with the Giants. At the tight end, Alvin Reed, now in his second year, should show the experience gained from a confusing and busy rookie season. Ed Carrington is also available and since both are 6 feet 5 inches and over 225 pounds, the Oilers' running game should also prosper.

Defensively, the Oilers are a solid ball club that points with pride to last year's accomplishments. They set AFL records for touchdowns scored against them, as well as points. This unit gave up only 18 touchdowns and held all opponents to less than 200 yards. Pat Holmes at defensive end is a master of the pass rush as well as being solid against the run. Watch him as he meets the interference on end runs and you'll see just how effective 260 pounds on a 6 feet 5 inch frame can be when it's used correctly. Gary Cutsinger is almost as effective as Holmes, although he is troubled by a chronic back condition.

Inside, the Oilers are just as solid, although much younger. Willie Parker is in his second year and he's as strong as they come. George Rice is the other tackle, and while not the biggest around, he has amazing quickness and agility.

Like all teams with good front fours, the Houston linebackers and secondary men come in for a great deal of praise and attention. In this case, however, the Oilers' two units deserve their plaudits. At the all-important middle-linebacking spot Garland Boyette has apparently found a home. It's hard to say what it is that makes a middle linebacker but whatever it is, Boyette has it. The two outsiders, all-pro George Webster and Olin Underwood, are perfect complements to Boyette.

All three are top-notch pass defenders (with good speed) and are especially effective with the complex red-dog defenses of Wally Lemm.

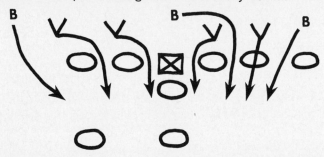

In the secondary, the Oilers have the AFL's best corner man in Miller Farr. Last year Farr picked off ten passes, an accomplishment that Farr laughs off and credits to his "hard-nosed" front four. But most of the AFL's coaches will tell you that, if they had their "druthers," they would rather not throw the ball around Farr.

Jim Norton at safety is another outstanding performer to watch in the Houston secondary. Norton is a nine-year veteran who contributes more than just physical skill to a secondary that picked off 26 passes last season.

In summation, if the Oilers can develop their passing game to the point of just being respectable, they could win it all. Beathard now in 1968 will be assuming a full-time starting role for the first time and he has proved he's capable.

The defense is there, so's the running game. Now if the Oilers could only throw the ball, Wally Lemm wouldn't have to worry much about "good losers."

HOUSTON OILERS   1968 Veterans Roster

NO.	NAME	POS.	HT.	WT.	AGE	YRS. IN PRO	COLLEGE
73	Allen, George	DT	6-7	275	24	2	West Texas State
58	Barnes, Pete	LB	6-3	245	22	2	Southern
27	Bass, Glenn	Flk	6-2	208	28	8	East Carolina
11	Beathard, Pete	QB	6-2	210	26	5	Southern California
71	Bernet, Lee	T	6-2	245	25	4	Wisconsin
66	Bishop, Sonny	G	6-2	245	28	7	Fresno State
42	Blanks, Sid	HB	6-0	208	26	4	Texas A&I
52	Boyette, Garland	LB	6-1	240	28	8	Grambling

NO.	NAME	POS.	HT.	WT.	AGE	YRS. IN PRO	COLLEGE
25	Burrell, Ode	Flk	6-0	195	27	5	Mississippi State
35	Campbell, Woodie	HB	5-11	205	24	2	Northwestern
41	Carwell, Larry	CB	6-1	190	23	2	Iowa State
51	Caveness, Ronnie	LB	6-1	225	25	4	Arkansas
80	Cutsinger, Gary	DE	6-4	250	28	6	Oklahoma State
12	Davis, Bob	QB	6-3	202	22	2	Virginia
26	Elkins, Lawrence	Flk	6-1	192	24	3	Baylor
20	Farr, Miller	CB	6-1	188	25	4	Wichita State
75	Floyd, Don	DE	6-3	245	28	9	TCU
28	Frazier, Charles	SE	6-0	188	28	7	Texas Southern
32	Granger, Hoyle	FB	6-1	225	23	3	Mississippi State
33	Hicks, W. K.	CB	6-1	190	26	5	Texas Southern
78	Hines, Glen Ray	T	6-5	270	24	3	Arkansas
79	Holmes, Pat	DE	6-5	260	27	5	Texas Tech
22	Hopkins, Roy	FB	6-1	227	23	2	Texas Southern
29	Houston, Ken	DB	6-3	192	23	2	Prairie View
21	Johns, Pete	DB	6-3	190	23	2	Tulane
50	Maples, Bobby	C	6-4	245	25	4	Baylor
62	Marcontell, Ed	G	6-0	240	22	2	Lamar Tech
77	Marshall, Richard	DT	6-4	270	27	4	Stephen F. Austin
63	Mitchell, Ed	G	6-3	275	26	3	Southern
22	Moore, Zeke	CB	6-2	190	24	2	Lincoln
43	Norton, Jim	DB	6-3	180	29	9	Idaho
74	Parker, Willie	DT	6-2	269	23	2	Arkansas AM&N
89	Reed, Alvin	TE	6-5	228	23	2	Prairie View
60	Regner, Tom	G	6-1	255	24	2	Notre Dame
72	Rice, George	DT	6-3	258	23	3	LSU
70	Stith, Carel	DE	6-5	270	22	2	Nebraska
76	Suggs, Walt	T	6-5	265	28	7	Mississippi State
87	Taylor, Lionel	SE	6-2	215	31	10	New Mexico Highlands
56	Underwood, Olen	LB	6-1	230	26	4	Texas
34	Viltz, Theo	DB	6-1	195	26	2	Southern California
90	Webster, George	LB	6-4	223	23	2	Michigan State
67	Wittenborn, John	Ki	6-2	240	31	11	Southeast Missouri

HOUSTON OILERS   1968 Top Rookies

NAME	POS.	HT.	WT.	AGE	COLLEGE	HOW ACQUIRED*
Beirne, Jim	S E	6-2	195	22	Purdue	D-4
Bethea, Elvin	G -T	6-3	255	22	N. Carolina A&T	D-3
Carrington, Ed	T E	6-4	220	24	Virginia	D-2
Longo, Bob	S E	6-4	210	22	Pittsburgh	D-5
Robertson, Bob	C	6-3½	232	21	Illinois	D-9
Toscano, Paul	D B	6-1	172	22	Wyoming	D-7

*D — Draft (Number indicates draft round)
FA — Free Agent

HOUSTON OILERS   1968 Schedule

Sept. 6 — Kansas City	7:30	Oct. 27 — at Buffalo	1:30
Sept. 14 — at Miami	8:00	Nov. 3 — at Cincinnati	1:30
Sept. 22 — at San Diego	1:00	Nov. 10 — at New York	1:30
Sept. 29 — Oakland	3:00	Nov. 17 — Denver	3:00
Oct. 6 — Miami	3:00	Nov. 28 — at Kansas City	12:30
Oct. 13 — at Boston	1:30	Dec. 7 — Buffalo	3:30
Oct. 20 — New York	3:00	Dec. 15 — Boston	3:00

MIAMI DOLPHINS

Coach George Wilson and his Miami Dolphins, if nothing else, can point with pride to the fact that in their first two years of existence, they won more games than any other expansion team during that same period. However, if pressed, the Dolphins must admit that their two-year total of victories adds up to only seven games. George Wilson is an "ole" pro, and he knows that his club, now in its third year, is still a long way from home. He has developed some outstanding talent in specific positions, but there are many areas that need help which just is not in sight.

Bob Griese is, and probably will be, the spark that will carry the Dolphins either up or down in 1968. He is an extremely versatile athlete and the kind of quarterback an expansion team needs, hard to get to and not easily hurt. Last year he stepped in when number-one man John Stofa broke his ankle in the very first game, and he compiled some rather impressive statistics.

Not only did Griese complete over 50 percent of his attempts for over 2,000 yards and 15 touchdowns, but at one point in the season had thrown 122 times without an interception. This to me tells a lot, and particularly about a rookie. There's nothing that hurts as much as an interception, and most rookies throw them with agonizing consistency. Griese doesn't, and he also directs with a flair an offense that, while still learning, can at times be explosive.

Another find for George Wilson was Jack Clancy at the split end. Clancy wound up on the receiving end of 67 passes last year, which is a credit not only to sound coaching, but to his own ability to learn the intricacies of the pro pass cuts. Clancy has good speed and like to run the fly and then fake the fly and catch the turn-in.

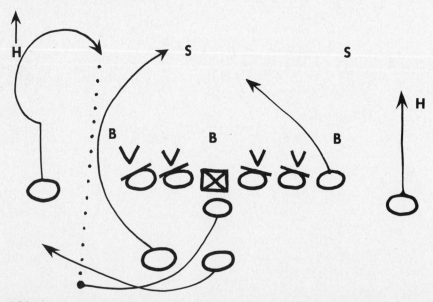

The Dolphins' running game (which wasn't a bad one last year) should gain even more stature this year with the addition of All-American Larry Csonka from Syracuse. Csonka is a tough "cookie" who can make his own holes, and with young teams this is often a necessity.

Csonka joins several other youngsters in what the Dolphins whimsically refer to as their "bubble-gum" backfield. Jack Harper and Stan Mitchell split most of the work last year, and they'll be back for more, as will flanker Howard Twilley.

Defensively, the Dolphins need just about what every team always looks for. Principally they need to improve this year on their pass rush. Mel Branch and Jim Riley do an adequate job at ends, but to win, and win consistently, you have to get to the quarterback, something which Miami does not major in.

In the secondary, Dick Westmoreland at right corner is the man to watch. He has what every corner back must have, speed, instincts, and the willingness to gamble. Last year he picked off ten enemy passes and that's without benefit of a great pass rush.

At linebacker, John Bramlett is the Dolphins' number-one red-dog man, a tactic that no one has more knowledge of than head coach George Wilson. The Dolphins are basically a four-three defense, and Bramlett comes on the dog from either inside or out, and usually in combination with his middle linebacker.

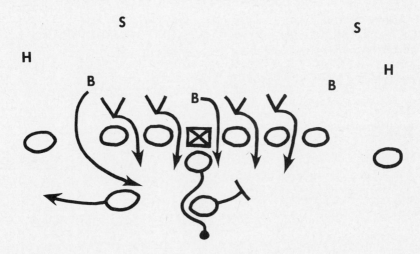

In summation, the Dolphins are a long way from home. However, they do play exciting football, and rookie Larry Csonka should spice that up even more. Griese and Clancy should continue to develop and there's no reason to believe they shouldn't become the winningest expansion team ever (over a three-year period, that is).

MIAMI DOLPHINS   1968 Veterans Roster

NO.	NAME	POS.	HT.	WT.	AGE	YRS. IN PRO	COLLEGE
32	Auer, Joe	HB	6-1	205	26	5	Georgia Tech
47	Beier, Tom	DB	5-11	198	22	1	Miami (Fla.)
57	Bramlett, John	LB	6-1	220	26	4	Memphis State
86	Branch, Mel	DE	6-1	235	31	8	LSU
56	Bruggers, Bob	LB	6-1	225	22	3	Minnesota
31	Chesser, George	FB	6-2	220	25	3	Delta State
24	Clancy, Jack	SE	6-1	195	23	1	Michigan
50	Emanuel, Frank	LB	6-3	225	25	3	Tennessee
53	Erlandson, Tom	LB	6-3	220	27	7	Washington State
71	Fowler, Charles	G-T	6-2	260	23	1	Houston
58	Goode, Tom	C	6-3	245	29	6	Mississippi State
12	Griese, Bob	QB	6-1	190	23	1	Purdue
29	Harper, Jack	HB	5-11	190	23	1	Florida
51	Hopkins, Jerry	LB	6-2	235	27	6	Texas A&M
26	Jackson, Frank	FL	6-1	185	28	8	SMU
84	Jacobs, Ray	DT	6-3	285	28	7	Howard Payne
5	Lusteg, Booth	K	5-10	190	28	3	Connecticut
54	McDaniel, Wahoo	LB-P	6-1	229	29	9	Oklahoma
—	Milton, Eugene (F.A.)	FL	5-10	170	23	R	Florida A&M
35	Mitchell, Stan	FB	6-2	220	23	3	Tennessee
82	Moreau, Doug	TE	6-1	205	23	3	LSU
43	Neff, Robert	DB	5-11	180	24	3	Stephen F. Austin
63	Neighbors, Billy	G	6-0	250	28	7	Alabama
76	Nomina, Tom	DT	6-3	260	25	6	Miami (Ohio)
89	Noonan, Karl	SE	6-3	190	24	3	Iowa
11	Norton, Rick	QB	6-2	190	24	3	Kentucky
48	Petrella, Bob	DB	6-0	185	23	3	Tennessee
30	Price, Sam	FB	5-11	215	24	3	Illinois
65	Pyburn, Jack	T	6-6	240	23	1	Texas A&M
74	Richardson, John	DT	6-2	250	22	2	UCLA
70	Riley, Jim	DE	6-4	240	22	1	Oklahoma
16	Roberts, Archie	QB	6-0	193	25	1	Columbia
23	Roderick, John	FL	6-0	180	23	3	SMU
20	Seiple, Larry	HB-P	6-0	200	23	1	Kentucky
59	Thornton, Jack	LB	6-1	228	23	3	Auburn
81	Twilley, Howard	FL	5-10	180	24	3	Tulsa
49	Warren, Jimmy	DB	5-11	175	28	5	Illinois
22	West, Willie	DB	5-10	185	29	9	Oregon
25	Westmoreland, Dick	DB	6-1	190	27	6	N. Carolina A&T
78	Williams, Maxie	T-G	6-4	250	27	4	S.E. Louisiana
61	Woodson, Freddie	G	6-2	250	23	1	Florida A&M

MIAMI DOLPHINS   1968 Top Rookies

NAME	POS.	HT.	WT.	AGE	COLLEGE	HOW ACQUIRED*
Anderson, Dick	D B-P	6-2	204	22	Colorado	D-3
Cox, Jim	T E	6-2	227	21	Miami	D-2
Crusan, Doug	O T	6-5	255	21	Indiana	D-1
Csonka, Larry	F B	6-3	235	21	Syracuse	D-1
Hammond, Kim	Q B	6-0	180	23	Florida State	D-6
Keyes, Jim	L B-PK	6-2	225	23	Mississippi	D-2
Kiick, Jim	H B	5-11	215	23	Wyoming	D-5
Urbanek, Jim	D T	6-4	250	22	Mississippi	D-3

*D — Draft (Number indicates draft round)
FA — Free Agent

MIAMI DOLPHINS   1968 Schedule

Sept. 14 — Houston	8:00	Nov. 3 — at San Diego	1:00
Sept. 21 — Oakland	8:00	Nov. 10 — at Buffalo	1:30
Sept. 28 — Kansas City	8:00	Nov. 17 — Cincinnati	1:30
Oct. 6 — at Houston	3:00	Nov. 24 — at Boston	1:30
Oct. 13 — Buffalo	1:30	Dec. 1 — at New York	1:30
Oct. 20 — at Cincinnati	1:30	Dec. 8 — Boston	1:30
Oct. 27 — at Denver	2:00	Dec. 15 — New York	1:30

NEW YORK JETS

The New York Jets are going into the 1968 AFL season looking back to what might have been in '67.

Last year the Jets came within one game of moving into an Eastern Division title, and while they don't make a practice of it, they could, with all honesty, say they blew a championship shot with the loss of one man, Emerson Boozer.

Boozer was on his way to an AFL record for touchdowns, as well as other league marks, when he suffered cartilage and ligament damage in the eighth game of the season.

This year, with the return of Emerson Boozer and a better year from Matt Snell, also coming off knee surgery, the Jets should be able to re-establish their running game to go with the best passing attack in the AFL.

Joe Namath and his receivers, Don Maynard, George Sauer, and Pete Lammons, were the league's best last year, and with the return of a running threat they should be better than ever.

Winston Hill and Sherman Plunkett at tackles, Dave Herman and Randy Rasmussen at guards, and John Schmidt at center do a fine job of protecting the weak-kneed Namath, who, given time to throw, displays the best arm in all of football.

Namath likes an assortment of passes (he threw 491 times last year) but he does have his favorites. Don Maynard is his touchdown threat, and like the Giants' Homer Jones, his best move is a fly pattern.

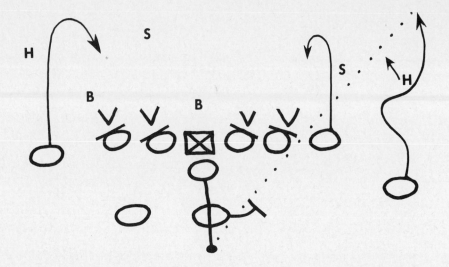

George Sauer, who led the league in receptions last year with 75, is Namath's clutch man and a good one at that. He doesn't possess the speed of Maynard, but probably has the better moves. On third-and-long situations, look for Namath to go with the following, the first to Sauer and the second to Maynard.

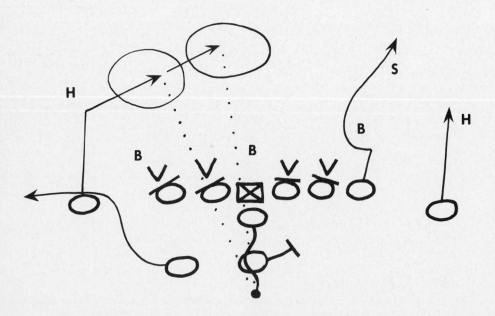

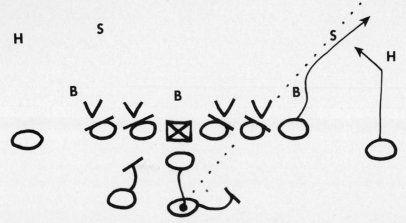

Defensively, the Jets are as solid as any team in the AFL, with the possible exception of their secondary. Their front four is a big one, headed by defensive end Verlon Biggs and Gerry Philbin.

Paul Rochester and John Elliott anchor the tackle spots, and they combined last year to limit such inside runners as Jim Nance and Hewritt Dixon to less than three yards per attempt.

But the real key to the Jets' defense lies in their linebacking. Larry Grantham and Ralph Baker play the corners, and Al Atkinson works in the middle. They can range deep to help a secondary (that often needs it) or they can become more than effective pass rushers with the red-dog. Here is where Grantham really shines, helping a defensive line that seems to have trouble rushing opposition passers.

The following is a defensive red-dog maneuver you can look for from Grantham on sure pass situations.

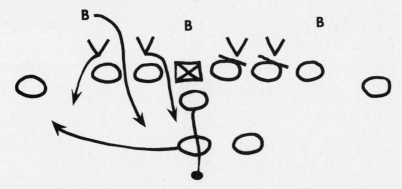

The Jets' secondary remains a problem for coach Weeb Ewbank. Randy Beverly moved in last year and did a fine job, but like his counterpart on the left side, Cornell Gordon, he can be beaten by the veteran receivers with quick sharp moves. Both cover well deep, but have trouble with those short third-down passes.

At safety, Billy Baird and Jim Hudson appear to be the best, but one or the other could be replaced by second-year man Henry King.

In summation, the Jets, if they stay healthy, could go all the way. They have their running game back, and this should allow Namath to avoid a record-breaking 28 interceptions, which he had last season.

Their defense is a solid four-three, with their linebackers making up for a lack of mobility by an otherwise tough front four.

NEW YORK JETS 1968 Veterans Roster

NO.	NAME	POS.	HT.	WT.	AGE	YRS. IN PRO	COLLEGE
62	Atkinson, Al	LB	6-2	228	25	4	Villanova
46	Baird, Bill	DB	5-10	180	29	6	San Francisco State
51	Baker, Ralph	LB	6-3	228	26	5	Penn State
42	Beverly, Randy	DB	5-11	185	24	2	Colorado State
86	Biggs, Verlon	DE	6-4	260	25	4	Jackson State
32	Boozer, Emerson	HB	5-11	207	25	3	Maryland State
77	Chomyszak, Steve	DT	6-5	275	24	2	Syracuse
45	Christy, Earl	DB	5-11	195	25	3	Maryland State
56	Crane, Paul	LB	6-2	205	24	3	Alabama
80	Elliott, John	DT-DE	6-4	245	22	2	Texas
48	Gordon, Cornell	DB	6-0	187	27	4	N. Carolina A&T
60	Grantham, Larry	LB	6-0	206	30	9	Mississippi
78	Harris, Jim	OT	6-4	280	25	4	Utah State
67	Herman, Dave	OG	6-1	255	27	5	Michigan State
75	Hill, Winston	OT	6-4	280	26	6	Texas Southern
22	Hudson, Jim	DB	6-2	210	25	4	Texas
35	Joe, Billy	FB	6-2	236	27	6	Villanova
33	Johnson, Curley	P-TE	6-0	215	33	11	Houston
40	King, Henry	DB	6-4	205	22	2	Utah State
87	Lammons, Pete	TE	6-3	228	24	3	Texas
31	Mathis, Bill	HB	6-1	220	29	9	Clemson
13	Maynard, Don	FL	6-1	179	31	11	Texas Western
50	McAdams, Carl	LB	6-3	240	24	2	Oklahoma
12	Namath, Joe	QB	6-2	195	25	4	Alabama
81	Philbin, Gerry	DE	6-2	248	27	5	Buffalo
79	Plunkett, Sherman	OT	6-2	330	34	11	Maryland State
23	Rademacher, Bill	DB	6-1	190	26	5	Northern Michigan
73	Randall, Dennis	DT	6-6	240	22	2	Oklahoma State
66	Rasmussen, Randy	OG	6-2	255	23	2	Kearney State
74	Richardson, Jeff	OG	6-3	260	23	2	Michigan State
72	Rochester, Paul	DT	6-2	255	30	9	Michigan State
24	Sample, John	DB	6-1	208	31	11	Maryland State
83	Sauer, George	OE	6-2	195	24	4	Texas
52	Schmitt, John	C	6-4	245	24	5	Hofstra
20	Schweickert, Bob	QB-FL	6-1	190	25	3	Virginia Tech
71	Seiler, Paul*	C-OT	6-4	255	21	2	Notre Dame
30	Smolinski, Mark	FB	6-1	215	29	8	Wyoming
41	Snell, Matt	FB	6-2	219	27	5	Ohio State
17	Taliaferro, Mike	QB	6-2	205	27	5	Illinois
29	Turner, Bake	OE	6-1	179	28	7	Texas Tech
11	Turner, Jim	K-QB	6-2	205	27	5	Utah State
82	Wilder, Bert	DT	6-3	245	28	5	N. Carolina State
88	Yearby, Bill	LB	6-3	235	24	2	Michigan

*In Military Service

NEW YORK JETS   1968 Top Rookies

NAME	POS.	HT.	WT.	AGE	COLLEGE	HOW ACQUIRED*
Jacobsen, Lee	T	6-2	210	22	Kearney State	D-5
Lubke, Oscar	T	6-4	255	24	Ball State	D-7
Magner, Gary	DT	6-3	230	22	Southern California	D-4
Thompson, Steve	D E-DT	6-5	245	22	Washington	D-2
Walton, Sam	T	6-5	262	25	East Texas State	D-3
White, Lee	FB	6-4	240	22	Weber State	D-1

*D — Draft (Number indicates draft round)
FA — Free Agent

NEW YORK JETS   1968 Schedule

Sept. 15 — at Kansas City	3:00	Nov. 3 — Buffalo	1:30
Sept. 22 — Boston (Birmingham)	2:00	Nov. 10 — Houston	1:30
Sept. 29 — at Buffalo	1:30	Nov. 17 — at Oakland	1:00
Oct. 5 — San Diego	8:00	Nov. 24 — at San Diego	1:00
Oct. 13 — Denver	1:30	Dec. 1 — Miami	1:30
Oct. 20 — at Houston	3:00	Dec. 8 — Cincinnati	1:30
Oct. 27 — Boston	1:30	Dec. 15 — at Miami	1:30

CINCINNATI BENGALS

When Paul Brown left the Cleveland Browns in 1963, he had compiled one of the most fantastic coaching records ever. For 13 years he had guided the Browns to an incredible 156 wins, while losing 42 and tying eight. Prior to that, he had been an even bigger winner in the old All-American Conference, taking the title in each of its four years of existence, while winning 42 games and losing only four.

The problems which now face Paul Brown in his initial year with the AFL's newest expansion team, the Bengals, could be described as "insurmountable," that is, if anyone but Paul Brown was at the helm.

The Bengals enter their first year of play with surplus players from each of the other AFL teams. Even though some of those players have relatively big names, you can't escape the fact that the reason they're with Cincinnati is that the team they were with last year didn't want them.

Some were players who were expendable because of general ability, others because of age or personality conflict with coaches or owners, and others lacked specific talents that their respective coaches felt were necessary to play pro football.

As a result of the increased expansion in pro football over the past years, the players Brown received from the other AFL teams and last year's draft are not as numerous or as talented as earlier expansion teams. This deduction is based on simple mathematics; there are just not that many players around. Paul Brown's monumental task is to now mold his crew of castoffs and youngsters into a representative football team.

In his pick of players from the expansion draft list, Brown went basically for youth and the good athlete rather than the specialist. One would assume from this, particularly if you've been a close observer of Paul Brown's career, that he wants to mold his own kind of football player. These players will learn over the years that Paul Brown is a demanding taskmaster, a perfectionist who will not tolerate less than total effort. They will also learn the fundamentals of football as well as they could from any coach, and while they will receive few plaudits from the "head man," if they have the ability and the desire, they will probably still be around when Paul Brown is once again a championship coach.

That day is a long way off, but it surely will come, and one has to assume that Brown will take the same road to success that he took with the Browns. His theory of football is basically quite simple. Obtain the best players and make them even better at specific assignments.

Offensively, his game with the Browns was one of equal parts of the run and the pass. His fullback will probably still control the running game, while you can look for him to develop outside receivers who are both physically talented and "smart."

Two big offensive plays for Paul Brown when he was directing the "old" Browns to one title after another were the following: first, the draw, which has now become a standard play with every team in football. The draw play

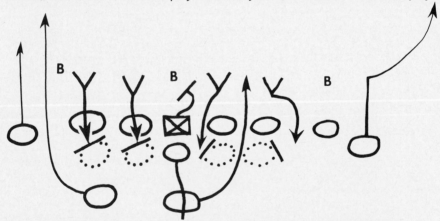

is designed to slow down a strong pass rush while also taking advantage of it. The offensive line sets as if to pass-block on the drop-back pass. As the over-eager defensive man "reads" pass and scrambles to get to the quarterback, he invariably is more off-balance than he would be were he being blocked straight away. It takes great timing by all players, as well as deceptive actions by the linemen and quarterbacks and fullback. All teams now use the draw, but you can bet the Bengals will use it with as much or more effectiveness as any other team.

Another play which Paul Brown brought to pro football is the "give," which, like the draw, is designed to take advantage of an over-eager defensive lineman.

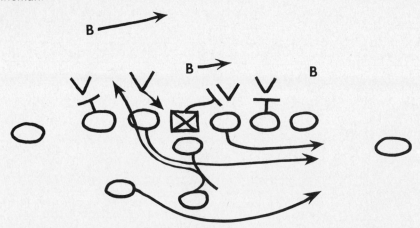

In the above, the offensive guard has pulled as if to lead a sweep to the right. The defensive tackle, seeing this, changes his charge to a pursuit angle. The quarterback has also opened as he does on a sweep and the fullback and halfback also take their initial sweep steps. The fullback, however, only takes the one jab step right, and then drives back hard, taking the ball and hitting the area vacated by the defensive lineman. No one blocks or touches the defensive lineman, and he usually comes back to the defensive huddle mumbling something to the effect, "What the hell happened?"

Paul Brown, who searched long and hard for his all-important quarterback, will begin his comeback with John Stofa, last year's number-one signal caller with the Miami Dolphins before suffering a broken leg. Stofa is big. He's 6 feet 3 inches and 210 pounds, and has shown he has what Paul Brown thinks makes up a top quarterback. He can run when he has to, can throw the ball long or deep, and has the intelligence that Brown feels is necessary for that position.

The Bengals' running game will probably be a combination of Bobby Burnett at halfback and Tom Smiley at fullback: Burnett, a former AFL rookie of the year in 1966 with Buffalo, and Smiley, the big (typical of Brown fullbacks) rookie from Lamar Tech.

The passing game, always of top caliber on a Paul Brown-coached team, will have as receivers Chris Burford, late of the Kansas City Chiefs, André White at tight end, and several flankers and split ends, Rod Sherman, Warren McVea, Elmo Maples, and Bob Trumpy.

Defensively, Bobby Hunt and Fletcher Smith, both acquired from Kansas City, offer some experience in the secondary to go with a lot of young, inexperienced speed.

The linebackers are headed by Sherrill Headrick, and one big job Paul Brown will have during 1968 is finding or developing that all-important middleman, a middle linebacker.

In summation, one would have to say the Bengals are in for some tough sledding. They have few if any potential super-stars, and their one hope is that they will be a team founded on successful principles and drilled to perfection.

For a while they are going to lose games because of physical ability, but they won't lose many because of lack of preparation or mental mistakes. Paul Brown is never under-prepared and he won't tolerate the mental error.

CINCINNATI BENGALS   1968 Veterans Roster

NAME	POS.	HT.	WT.	AGE	YRS. IN PRO	COLLEGE	HOW ACQUIRED*
Archer, Dan	T	6-5	250	23	2	Oregon	Exp
Bailey, Bill	FB	6-0	222	23	3	Cincinnati	FA
Banks, Estes	HB	6-3	215	22	2	Colorado	Exp
Bellino, Joe	FL	5-9	185	29	4	Navy	Exp
Bitsko, Mickey	LB	6-0	232	25	2	Dayton	FA
Boudreaux, Jim	T	6-4	250	24	3	Louisiana Tech.	Exp
Brabham, Danny	LB	6-3	240	26	6	Arkansas	Exp
Brannan, Solomon	DB	6-0	182	24	4	Morris Brown	Exp
Brownlee, Claude	DT	6-5	270	24	2	Benedict	FA
Buncom, Frank	LB	6-1	242	27	7	Southern California	Exp
Burford, Chris	SE	6-2	215	29	9	Stanford	Exp
Burnett, Bobby	HB	6-2	205	24	3	Arkansas	Exp
Clay, Ozzie	DB	6-0	196	25	4	Iowa State	FA
Garrett, J. D.	FL	5-11	190	26	5	Grambling	Exp
Graves, White	DB	6-0	185	24	4	LSU	Exp
Griffin, Jim	DE	6-3	260	25	4	Grambling	Exp
Hall, Ron	DB	6-0	190	30	9	Missouri Valley	Exp
Headrick, Sherrill	LB	6-1	235	31	10	TCU	Exp
Hunt, Bobby	DB	6-1	185	28	7	Auburn	Exp
Isbell, Joe Bob	G	6-1	240	27	5	Houston	Exp
Jones, Willie Lee	DE	6-3	255	25	2	Kansas State	Exp
Kellogg, Mike	FB	6-0	228	24	3	Santa Clara	Exp
King, Charlie	DB	6-0	186	25	3	Purdue	Exp
Lucka, Rich	G	6-1	245	25	2	Cincinnati	FA
Marsh, Frank	HB	6-2	205	27	2	Oregon State	Exp
Matlock, John	C	6-3	246	23	2	Miami	Exp
Matson, Pat	G	6-4	250	23	3	Oregon	Exp
Perreault, Pete	G	6-3	245	27	7	Boston U.	Exp
Petrich, Bob	DE	6-4	252	27	6	West Texas State	FA
Poole, Bob	TE	6-4	220	26	5	Clemson	Exp
Reynolds, Al	G	6-3	250	29	9	Tarkio	Exp
Rice, Andy	DT	6-2	260	26	3	Texas Southern	Exp
Roy, Frank	G	6-3	245	24	3	Utah	FA
Schmidt, Bob	C	6-4	240	31	10	Minnesota	Exp
Sherman, Rod	FL	6-0	190	23	2	Southern California	Exp
Sligh, Richard	DT	7-0	300	22	2	N. Carolina College	Exp
Smith, Fletcher	DB	6-0	188	24	3	Tennessee State	Exp
Sorrell, Henry	LB	6-1	230	23	2	Chattanooga	Exp
Stofa, John	QB	6-3	210	25	3	Buffalo	Trade
Van Raaphorst, Dick	PK	5-11	215	25	4	Ohio State	Exp
Waskiewicz, Jim	DT	6-3	250	23	3	Wichita State	Exp
White, Andre	TE	6-3	225	23	2	Florida A&M	Trade
Williams, Don	SE	6-5	218	23	2	Akron	FA
Wright, Ernie	T	6-4	270	29	9	Ohio State	Exp
Wright, Lonnie	DB	6-2	205	23	3	Colorado State	Exp
Zecher, Rich	DT	6-2	255	24	4	Utah State	Exp

*No numbers have yet been assigned the players.
Exp indicates "expansion"
FA — Free Agent

CINCINNATI BENGALS   1968 Rookie Roster

NAME	POS.	HT.	WT.	AGE	COLLEGE	HOW ACQUIRED*
Anders, Billy	SE	6-2	196	22	Ohio State	FA
Banks, Jeff	LB	6-1	235	22	University of Pacific	D-11
Bean, Wesley	LB	6-2	220	22	Grambling	D-7
Beauchamp, Al	DE	6-2	240	23	Southern U.	D-5
Birkley, Dain	DB	6-1	192	21	Denison	FA
Bivins, James	LB	6-2	230	23	Texas Southern	D-13
Brantley, Ed	T	6-5	255	22	North Texas State	D-8
Brooks, Chuck	T	6-5	250	25	Memphis State	FA
Brown, Bill	T	6-4	255	25	Texas (El Paso)	Exp
Cairns, Gary	PK	6-1	210	23	Ohio State	FA
Carr, Leon	LB	6-3	230	24	Prairie View	FA
Catavalos, George	DB	6-1	195	23	Purdue	FA
Clay, Leonard	DB	5-10	190	23	Maryland State	FA
Clemons, Mike	LB-PK	6-0	230	22	Sacramento	FA
Collier, Pat	LB	6-2	225	23	North Central	FA
Curry, Jim	TE	6-4	220	25	Cincinnati	FA
Danielson, Darrel	PK	5-9	190	22	Idaho	FA
Davis, Gary	QB	6-2	205	23	Vanderbilt	D-3
Echols, Fate	G	6-2	260	25	Northwestern	FA
Ellis, Sidney	DB	6-0	185	22	Jackson State	D-6
Fest, Howard	T	6-5	245	22	Texas	D-6
Frazier, Curt	DB	5-11	188	23	Fresno State	FA
Gunner, Harry	DE	6-5	243	23	Oregon State	D-8
Hanrahan, Steve	DT	6-5	260	22	Weber State	D-9
Hoose, Jim	SE	6-1	197	23	Cincinnati	FA
Hoovler, Don	LB	6-2	230	25	Ohio U.	FA
Johns, Nate	HB	6-0	188	23	San Diego State	Exp
Johnson, Bob	C	6-5	245	21	Tennessee	D-1
Johnson, Essex	DB	6-2	235	22	Grambling	D-6
Johnson, James	DB	6-1	204	22	South Carolina	D-6
Jones, Harold	G	6-3	245	22	Grambling	D-12
Jones, Lionel	SE	6-1	190	23	Southern U.	FA
Keeling, Rex	PK	6-3	200	24	Stamford	FA
Kindricks, Bill	DT	6-4	265	21	Alabama A&M	D-6
Kennerly, Tom	SE	6-2	199	21	S. Carolina State	FA
Lewicke, Steve	DE	6-2	240	21	Texas (El Paso)	D-14
Livingston, Dale	PK-PT	6-0	220	21	Western Michigan	D-3
Mackey, Billy	SE	6-1	210	24	Bakersfield	FA
Manning, Don	LB	6-2	220	21	UCLA	D-17
Maples, Elmo	SE	6-1	190	22	Southern U.	D-6
Marks, Brown	LB	6-2	220	19	Indiana	D-16
McVea, Warren	FL	5-9	185	21	Houston	D-4
Middendorf, Dave	G	6-3	255	22	Washington State	D-5
Mira, Joe	FL	6-1	190	22	Miami	D-15
Neidert, John	LB	6-2	240	22	Louisville	D-6
Palmore, Harvey	G	6-2	260	23	Morgan State	D-15
Patrick, Wayne	FB	6-1	230	21	Louisville	D-10
Peterson, Bill	TE	6-2	230	23	San Jose State	FA
Phillips, Jess	HB	6-2	205	22	Michigan State	D-4
Reynolds, Roger	SE	6-1	193	25	Bowling Green	FA
Rhoads, Tom	LB	6-2	240	22	Notre Dame	Trade
Robinson, Paul	HB	6-0	198	23	Arizona	D-3
Rooney, Hal	DHB	6-2	185	23	Syracuse	FA
Saffold, D. T.	SE	6-4	202	24	San Jose State	FA
Scott, Bill	DB	6-0	188	23	Idaho	FA
Scott, Wally	DB	6-0	190	22	Arizona	D-11

135

NAME	POS.	HT.	WT.	AGE	COLLEGE	HOW ACQUIRED*
Seals, Tom	DT-PK	6-4	260	23	Georgetown	FA
Shear, Bill	PK	6-0	180	23	Cortland State	FA
Smiley, Tom	FB	6-1	235	23	Lamar Tech	D-2
Smith, Jim	TE	6-1	230	23	Jackson State	D-17
Smith, Steve	TE	6-2	240	22	Miami	D-7
Staley, Bill	DE	6-3	248	21	Utah State	D-2
Thornton, William	SE	6-0	185	25	Utah State	FA
Trumpy, Bob	SE	6-5	215	22	Utah	D-12
Van Pelt, Bob	C	6-2	240	24	Indiana	FA
Warren, Dewey	QB	6-0	206	22	Tennessee	D-6
Watts, Claude	HB	6-0	212	25	Bloomfield State	FA
Webster, Les	HB	6-0	200	22	Iowa State	D-14
Whitehead, Dennis	DB	6-1	175	25	Miami (Ohio)	FA
Wilfork, Roy	LB	6-2	228	26	Missouri Valley	FA
Williams, James	DB	6-1	190	23	Alcorn A&M	D-16
Williams, Monk	FL	5-7	155	23	Arkansas A&M	D-6
Wise, Eddie	DB	5-10	180	24	None	FA
Wyche, Sam	QB	6-3	210	23	Furman	FA

*D-Draft (Number indicates draft round)
FA-Free Agent
Exp-Acquired in expansion draft.

CINCINNATI BENGALS   1968 Schedule

Sept. 9 — at San Diego	6:00	Oct. 27 — at Oakland	1:00
Sept. 15 — Denver	1:30	Nov. 3 — Houston	1:30
Sept. 22 — Buffalo	1:30	Nov. 10 — Kansas City	1:30
Sept. 29 — San Diego	1:30	Nov. 17 — at Miami	1:30
Oct. 6 — at Denver	2:00	Nov. 24 — Oakland	1:30
Oct. 13 — at Kansas City	3:00	Dec. 1 — at Boston	1:30
Oct. 20 — Miami	1:30	Dec. 8 — at New York	1:30

DENVER BRONCOS

When Lou Saban took over the Denver Broncos, he knew that the task ahead was a monumental one.

The Broncos were losers and before you do anything with a losing football team, you must change the attitude. Saban feels the Broncos did just that in 1967, even though they were on the short end of a three and eleven record.

It was a year of evaluation for Saban who earlier in his career turned the Buffalo Bills, another also-ran, into a championship team. Saban made those evaluations, and then made some dramatic decisions. He tabbed quarterback Steve Tensi as the man to run his offense, and stuck with it. Now, Tensi, who has had a short and spotted career, is developing into a very capable quarterback.

When he arrived at Denver from San Diego, his specialty was just rearing back and letting fire. He was big and strong, à la Roman Gabriel, but thoroughly lacked the finesse for the short game. Toward the end of last season, Tensi, under Saban's direction, began to put the long and the short together. He wound up the number-one man and threw for 16 touchdowns while completing 131 of 325 attempts.

The Broncos' running game centers around rugged little Floyd Little, a second-year "package" out of Syracuse. He's deceptively fast and resembles Mike Garrett a great deal. The Broncos try to get Little into an open field, where his shiftiness gives him a decided edge over tacklers. One way the Broncos do this is with the flare screen.

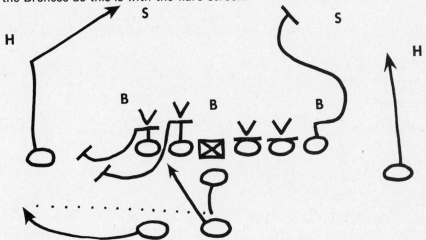

Another play that the Broncos will use to get Little into an open field is the screen pass.

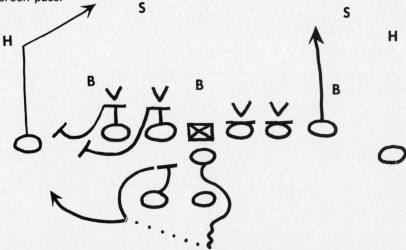

Al Denson and Eric Crabtree are the Broncos' number-one and -two receiving specialists, along with tight end Tom Beer. Crabtree and Denson can both go for the bomb, with all-pro Crabtree usually getting the call on third-and-must situations.

In the offensive line, the Broncos need help and know it. Larry Kaminski is solid at center, but rookie linemen Bob Hendrix and Bob Vaughn are going to get a lot of early-season trial.

On defense, tackle Dave Costa is head and shoulders over his running mates. At a squat 6 feet 1 inch and 260 pounds, he is a terror against the run while amazingly mobile as a pass rusher. Jerry Inman and end Dick Jackson both have shown promise in Saban's master plan, with Jackson now in his second year away from linebacking a definite bright spot.

In the secondary, the Broncos also need help. As a matter of fact, Saban openly admits that this is where he is hurting the most. Two starters from last year, safety Jack Lentz and corner man Nemish Wilson, are back, but rookies Frank Loria and Drake Garrett, along with second-year man Tom Cassese, could likely be starters before the season ends.

In summation, the Broncos need help in many areas. Their secondary must continue to improve, as must their linebacking. Steve Tensi must continue to show Saban that he justifies his role as starter, and if the Broncos are going to score points they will have to keep Floyd Little healthy.

DENVER BRONCOS   1968 Veterans Roster

NO.*	NAME	POS.	HT.	WT.	AGE	YRS. IN PRO	COLLEGE
	Andrus, Lou	LB	6-6	255	24	2	Brigham Young
	Beer, Tom	OE	6-4	235	22	2	Houston
	Brunelli, Sam	OT	6-1	255	23	3	Colorado State
	Cassese, Tom	DB	6-1	197	21	2	C. W. Post
	Cichowski, Tom	OT	6-4	250	22	2	Maryland
	Costa, Dave	DT	6-1	265	25	6	Utah
	Cox, Larry	DT	6-2	250	23	3	Abilene Christian
	Crabtree, Eric	OE	5-11	182	22	3	Pittsburgh
	Cunningham, Carl	LB	6-3	241	22	2	Houston
	Current, Mike	OT	6-1	250	21	2	Ohio State
	Daniels, Dave	DT	6-4	265	27	3	Florida A&M
	Denson, Al	OE	6-2	208	25	5	Florida A&M
	Duranko, Pete	DE	6-2	240	23	2	Notre Dame
	Goeddeke, George	G	6-3	240	22	2	Notre Dame
	Hickey, Bo	OB	5-11	225	21	2	Maryland
	Huard, John	LB	6-0	220	22	2	Maine
	Humphreys, Bob	K	6-1	240	27	2	Wichita State
	Inman, Jerry	DT	6-3	255	27	3	Oregon
	Jackson, Richard	DE	6-3	255	25	3	Southern
	Jaquess, Pete	DB	5-11	182	28	4	Eastern New Mexico
	Kaminski, Larry	C	6-2	240	22	3	Purdue
	Leclair, Jim	QB	6-1	207	23	2	C. W. Post
	Leclerc, Roger	C	6-2	245	30	9	Trinity (Conn.)
	Leetzow, Max	DE	6-4	255	23	4	Idaho
	Lentz, Jack	DB	6-0	195	22	2	Holy Cross
	Little, Floyd	OB	5-10	195	25	2	Syracuse
	Lynch, Fran	OB	6-1	210	23	2	Hofstra
	Maddox, John	DE	6-4	250	25	2	Mississippi
	Mirich, Rex	DE	6-4	250	26	5	Northern Arizona
	Mitchell, Charlie	OB	5-11	185	27	5	Washington
	Myrtle, Charles	LB	6-2	215	22	2	Maryland
	Park, Ernie	G	6-3	240	26	6	McMurry
	Ply, Bobby	DB	6-1	190	27	7	Baylor

NO.*	NAME	POS.	HT.	WT.	AGE	YRS. IN PRO	COLLEGE
	Richter, Frank	LB	6-3	230	22	2	Georgia
	Sbranti, Ron	LB	6-2	230	22	3	Utah State
	Scarpitto, Bob	OE-P	5-11	196	28	8	Notre Dame
	Summers, Jim	DB	5-10	175	21	2	Michigan State
	Sweeney, Neal	OE	6-2	170	22	2	Tulsa
	Tensi, Steve	QB	6-5	215	24	4	Florida State
	Tyson, Dick	G	6-2	245	24	3	Tulsa
	Wilson, Nemiah	DB	6-0	165	24	4	Grambling
	Young, Bob	OG	6-2	260	24	3	Howard Payne

*Numbers not yet assigned.

DENVER BRONCOS   1968 Top Rookies

NAME	POS.	HT.	WT.	AGE	COLLEGE	HOW ACQUIRED*
Culp, Curley	DT	6-1	255	21	Arizona State	D-1
Ford, Garrett	OB	6-2½	230	22	West Virginia	D-2
Garrett, Drake	DB	5-9	185	21	Notre Dame	D-5
Holloman, Gus	DB	6-2	190	21	Houston	D-6
Lambert, Gordon	DE	6-5	237	22	Tennessee	D-4

*D — Draft (Number indicates draft round)
FA — Free Agent

DENVER BRONCOS   1968 Schedule

Sept. 15 — at Cincinnati	1:30		Nov. 3 — at Boston	1:30
Sept. 22 — at Kansas City	3:00		Nov. 10 — Oakland	1:00
Sept. 29 — Boston	2:00		Nov. 17 — at Houston	3:00
Oct. 6 — Cincinnati	2:00		Nov. 24 — Buffalo	2:00
Oct. 13 — at New York	1:30		Dec. 1 — San Diego	2:00
Oct. 20 — at San Diego	1:00		Dec. 8 — at Oakland	1:00
Oct. 27 — Miami	2:00		Dec. 14 — Kansas City	2:00

KANSAS CITY CHIEFS

Head coach Hank Stram is faced with tremendous rebuilding problems this season. He's lost six players who were regular starters last year, and it's hard to conceive how the Chiefs can regain their late-season form of last year, at least in the early going.

A couple of position changes have helped the Chiefs a great deal. E. J. Holub has moved from linebacker to center, where the wear and tear on a pair of questionable knees will not be so severe, and Chuck Hurston has moved from the defensive line to linebacker. This of course means the two vacated areas will be weaker, but it's in these positions Stram feels he has at least some potential.

The secondary has also been weakened. Starters Freddie Williamson and Fletcher Smith are gone, and Stram, through necessity, will have to go with youth in this all-important unit. Emmitt Thomas and Goldie Sellers are the two prime candidates to fill in here.

However, it isn't all gloom for the Chiefs. Much of the defensive unit is back, and they have some good ones. Big Buck Buchanan, Jerry Mays, and Ernie Ladd are big cogs in a front four that two years ago was the best in the AFL. Bobby Bell at linebacker is more than capable, and Willie Mitchell at corner and Johnny Robinson at safety are both experienced and can handle the Chiefs' multiple defenses.

On offense, the Chiefs have also lost some key men (receiver Chris Burford and center Jon Gilliam), but they retain the heart of an explosive scoring unit headed by Lennie Dawson at quarterback and Mike Garrett at halfback.

Dawson is the AFL's all-time leading passer, and I guess you would have to say he is also the AFL's counterpart of the NFL's Fran Tarkenton. He's a scrambler deluxe, and because of it can often get a pass off that other quarterbacks could not.

Garrett is Dawson's principal offensive weapon. Last year, the little USC fireplug finished in the AFL's top ten as both a passer and a rusher. He is almost impossible for one man to bring down in the open field, and consequently Dawson likes to get him outside as quickly as possible.

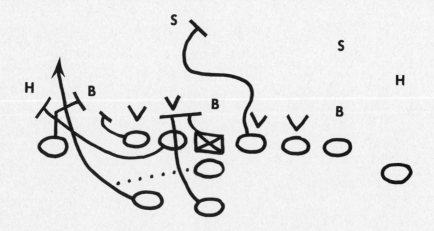

Another way to get Garrett into a broken field is by the use of the screen pass. Dawson is good at this because he can fake a scramble, pulling the defensive line back with him, and then flip softly over their heads to Garrett, waiting behind the offensive convoy.

140

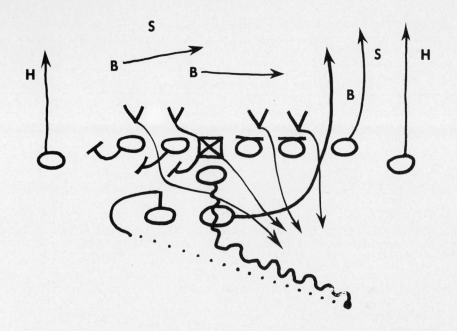

Curtis McClinton is now the Chiefs' main threat as a receiver. He has some of the fine moves in the game today, with his sideline pattern perhaps

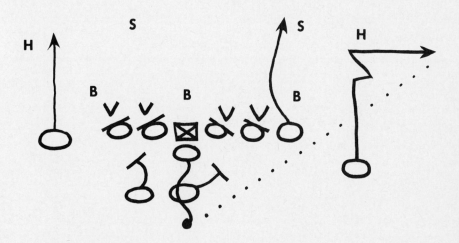

the best. McClinton also has a takeoff on the sideline which he and Dawson have timed out to near perfection.

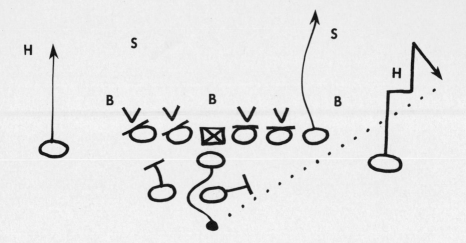

In summation, one would have to say that head coach Hank Stram is going to need some really outstanding come-through performances by rookies and veterans playing in strange positions if his club is going to be a contender. It's hard to conceive of a team losing what the Chiefs have and still maintaining a winning consistency. Nevertheless, Hank Stram is a fine, inventive coach, and you can expect he'll do the best with what is available.

KANSAS CITY CHIEFS   1968 Veterans Roster

NO.	NAME	POS.	HT.	WT.	AGE	YRS. IN PRO	COLLEGE
52	Abell, Bud	LB	6-3	220	27	3	Missouri
84	Arbanas, Fred	E	6-3	240	29	7	Michigan State
78	Bell, Bobby	LB	6-4	228	28	6	Minnesota
61	Biodrowski, Dennis	G	6-1	255	28	6	Memphis State
87	Brown, Aaron	DE	6-5	265	24	2	Minnesota
86	Buchanan, Buck	DT	6-7	287	28	6	Grambling
71	Budde, Ed	G	6-5	260	27	6	Michigan State
80	Carolan, Reg	E	6-6	240	28	7	Idaho
23	Coan, Bert	HB	6-4	220	28	7	Kansas
16	Dawson, Len	QB	6-0	190	33	12	Purdue
72	DiMidio, Tony	T	6-3	250	26	3	West Chester State
76	Dotson, Alphonse	DT	6-4	260	25	3	Grambling
66	Frazier, Wayne	C	6-3	245	29	5	Auburn
21	Garrett, Mike	HB	5-9	200	24	3	Southern California
38	Hayes, Wendell	HB	6-1	195	26	4	Humboldt State
73	Hill, Dave	T	6-5	260	27	6	Auburn
55	Holub, E. J.	C	6-4	236	30	8	Texas Tech
54	Hudock, Mike	C	6-2	245	34	10	Miami (Fla.)
85	Hurston, Chuck	LB	6-6	240	25	4	Auburn
46	Kearney, Jim	DB	6-2	206	25	4	Prairie View
70	Kelly, Bobby	T	6-4	265	27	5	New Mexico State
58	Kubala, Ray	C	6-4	245	25	5	Texas A&M
99	Ladd, Ernie	DT	6-9	290	29	8	Grambling
63	Lanier, Willie	LB	6-1	245	23	1	Morgan State
15	Lee, Jacky	QB	6-1	185	29	9	Cincinnati
48	Longmire, Sam	FL	6-3	195	25	1	Purdue
52	Lothamer, Ed	DT	6-5	270	25	5	Michigan State

NO.	NAME	POS.	HT.	WT.	AGE.	YRS. IN PRO	COLLEGE
51	Lynch, Jim	LB	6-1	235	23	1	Notre Dame
75	Mays, Jerry	DE	6-4	252	28	8	SMU
32	McClinton, Curtis	FB	6-3	227	28	7	Kansas
64	Merz, Curt	G	6-4	267	30	9	Iowa
22	Mitchell, Willie	DB	6-0	185	28	5	Tennessee A&I
25	Pitts, Frank	E	6-2	199	24	4	Southern
65	Prudhomme, Remi	DT	6-4	250	26	3	LSU
30	Richardson, Gloster	E	6-0	200	25	1	Jackson State
42	Robinson, Johnny	DB	6-1	205	30	9	LSU
20	Sellers, Goldie	DB	6-2	198	26	3	Grambling
1	Smith, Noland	FL	5-8	163	24	1	Tennessee State
3	Stenerud, Jan	K	6-2	187	25	1	Montana State
89	Taylor, Otis	FL	6-3	215	26	4	Prairie View
18	Thomas, Emmitt	DB	6-2	192	25	3	Bishop
74	Trosch, Gene	DE	6-7	277	23	1	Miami (Fla.)
77	Tyrer, Jim	T	6-6	292	29	8	Ohio State
12	Walker, Wayne	K	6-2	215	23	2	Northwest Louisiana
44	Wilson, Jerrel	K	6-4	222	25	6	Southern Mississippi

KANSAS CITY CHIEFS   1968 Top Rookies

NAME	POS.	HT.	WT.	AGE	COLLEGE	HOW ACQUIRED*
Daney, George	G	6-3½	240	21	Texas	D-1a
Grezaffi, Sam	D B	5-10	175	21	LSU	D-7
Livingston, Mike	Q B	6-3	205	22	SMU	D-2
McCarty, Mickey	T E	6-5	255	21	TCU	D-3
Moorman, Maurice	G	6-5	252	23	Texas A&M	D-1

*D — Draft (Number indicates draft round)
FA — Free Agent

KANSAS CITY CHIEFS   1968 Schedule

Sept. 6 — at Houston	7:30	Oct. 27 — San Diego	3:00
Sept. 15 — New York	3:00	Nov. 3 — at Oakland	1:00
Sept. 22 — Denver	3:00	Nov. 10 — at Cincinnati	1:30
Sept. 28 — at Miami	8:00	Nov. 17 — Boston	3:00
Oct. 5 — at Buffalo	8:00	Nov. 28 — Houston	12:30
Oct. 13 — Cincinnati	3:00	Dec. 8 — at San Diego	1:00
Oct. 20 — Oakland	3:00	Dec. 14 — at Denver	2:00

OAKLAND RAIDERS

The Oakland Raiders, the defending champions of the AFL, are one of the most solid, well-balanced teams in all of pro football. AFL Coach of the Year Johnny Rauch and his predecessor Al Davis have assembled a young team that is going to be around for a long time to come.

The Raiders have name stars, like all great teams, but the overall strength of the club is not based on one, two, or even several of its members. They are a young group that, following last year's loss to the Green Bay Packers for the world championship, realized they belong on the field with the best. They were beaten in that second Super Bowl game, but they were not beaten up. As a matter of fact, only a couple of miscues kept the score from being a lot closer than it was.

Daryle Lamonica is back at the key quarterback position, deservedly wearing his "player-of-the-year" honors. Lamonica, who came into his own last year, has the all-around versatility that the modern quarterback needs. He is a fine passer, short and deep, and can scramble when in trouble.

He guides a well-balanced running game, featuring fullback Hewritt Dixon and halfbacks Clem Daniels and Pete Banaszak. Dixon is the key man in the Raiders' running game, and a big feature of their passing game. A former tight end before moving to the backfield, at 6 feet 1 inch and 220 pounds, he has developed into one of the most versatile backs in pro football. He runs best inside, behind a veteran offensive line that can give him that inch of daylight, which is all a big back needs.

Jim Otto is the key man in that five-man front. Otto is flanked by guards Wayne Hawkins and Gene Upshaw and tackles Henry Schuh and Bob Svihus. They're big, young, and do a lot of things well, such as opening the off-tackle holes for Dixon.

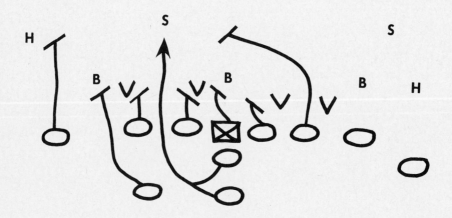

When the Raiders want to go outside, they can send Clem Daniels or Pete Banaszak on the sweep, with Daniels, coming off a broken ankle, the better of the two. The Raiders like the sweep on first and ten, and third and medium yardage.

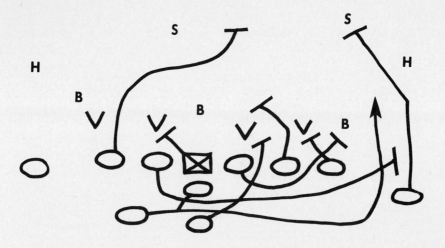

Oakland's offensive line is also one of the best at protecting quarterback Daryle Lamonica. With this strong pass protection, Lamonica can use not only his three up-front receivers, but can send his set backs into the pattern. Dixon led the Raiders last year in receptions, and while he usually is involved in the short game, he often turns a reception into a big gain with his running ability.

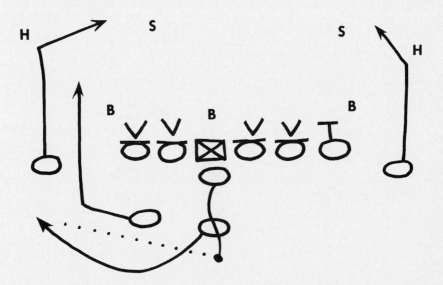

Lamonica likes to use the double flanker and variations of the same to assure getting his receivers into man-to-man defensive situations. The following is one pattern he will use to get Bill Miller one-on-one with a tight safety.

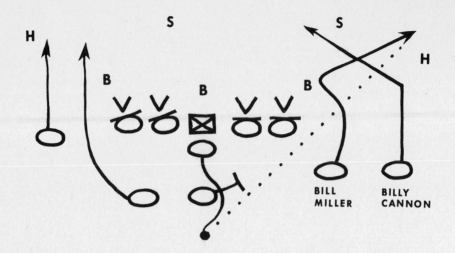

Tight end Billy Cannon is also a clutch third-and-long-yardage receiver for Lamonica. The following is one of several patterns Cannon, a former running back, will use.

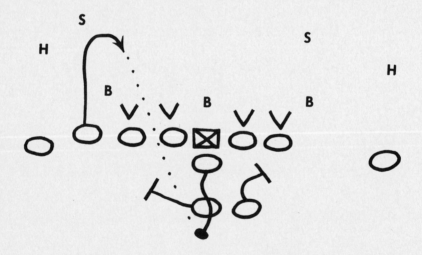

Defensively, the Raiders are the equal of any team in the AFL. Up front, they are big and quick. Ben Davidson is the most renowned, but Tom Keating and Dan Birdwell are just as effective because of their incredible quickness. The Raiders operate mainly from the four-three, although they will use a five-man front overshifting to the opposition's strong side.

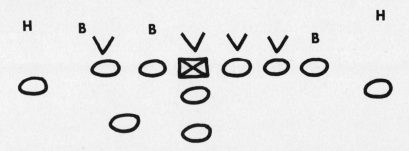

The Raiders' linebacking corps is a solid one, headed by Gus Otto, Dan Connors, and Bill Laskey, a former teammate of mine with the New York Giants. They are extremely mobile and can range deep to help the secondary, or can come with the red-dog as effectively as any team in the AFL.

The Raiders' secondary is a young, fast, and improving unit. Last year in the Super Bowl they were victimized by the play-calling of Green Bay's Bart Starr (but, then, who hasn't been?). Kent McCloughan, Willie Brown, Dave Grayson, and Rodger Bird are the key men, and like all teams with a strong pass rush, they can afford to play a tight man to man.

In summation, the Raiders are going to be the kings of the AFL for some-time to come, providing they can avoid an epidemic of injuries. They have balance, and now, after their fine showing against Green Bay, they have confidence. Look for the Raiders to play their second consecutive Super Bowl in January.

OAKLAND RAIDERS   1968 Veterans Roster

NO.	NAME	POS.	HT.	WT.	AGE	YRS. IN PRO	COLLEGE
40	Banaszak, Pete	OB	5-11	200	24	3	Miami (Fla.)
64	Behrman, David	C	6-5	265	26	5	Michigan State
50	Benson, Duane	LB	6-2	215	22	2	Hamline
25	Biletnikoff, Fred	OE	6-1	190	25	4	Florida State
21	Bird, Rodger	DB	5-11	195	24	3	Kentucky
53	Birdwell, Dan	DT	6-4	250	27	7	Houston
16	Blanda, George	QB	6-3	215	40	19	Kentucky
24	Brown, Willie	DB	6-1	190	27	6	Grambling
48	Budness, Bill	LB	6-2	215	25	5	Boston U.
33	Cannon, Billy	OE	6-1	215	30	9	LSU
55	Conners, Dan	LB	6-1	230	26	5	Miami (Fla.)
80	Cook, Ed	DE	6-4	245	32	11	Maryland
36	Daniels, Clem	OB	6-1	218	30	9	Prairie View A&M
83	Davidson, Ben	DE	6-7	265	27	8	Washington
19	Davidson, Cotton	QB	6-0	180	36	12	Baylor
35	Dixon, Hewritt	OB	6-1	220	28	6	Florida A&M
11	Eischeid, Mike	K	6-0	190	27	3	Upper Iowa
86	Fairband, Bill	LB	6-3	228	22	2	Colorado

NO.	NAME	POS.	HT.	WT.	AGE	YRS. IN PRO	COLLEGE
45	Grayson, Dave	DB	5-10	185	28	8	Oregon
12	Green, Charlie	QB	6-0	190	24	2	Wittenberg
30	Hagberg, Roger	OB	6-1	215	29	7	Minnesota
70	Harvey, James	G	6-5	245	24	3	Mississippi
65	Hawkins, Wayne	G	6-0	240	29	9	Pacific
84	Herock, Ken	OE	6-2	230	26	5	West Virginia
71	Keating, Bill	DT	6-2	236	23	3	Michigan
74	Keating, Tom	DT	6-2	247	25	5	Michigan
88	Kocourek, Dave	OE	6-5	240	30	10	Wisconsin
62	Kruse, Bob	G	6-2	250	23	2	Wayne State (Neb.)
3	Lamonica, Daryle	QB	6-3	215	26	6	Notre Dame
42	Laskey, Bill	LB	6-3	235	25	4	Michigan
77	Lassiter, Isaac	DE	6-5	270	27	7	St. Augustine
47	McCloughan, Kent	DB	6-1	190	25	4	Nebraska
89	Miller, Bill	OE	6-0	190	28	7	Miami (Fla.)
85	Oats, Carleton	DE	6-2	235	26	4	Florida A&M
34	Otto, Gus	LB	6-2	220	24	4	Missouri
00	Otto, Jim	C	6-2	240	30	9	Miami (Fla.)
75	Park, Ernie	OG	6-3	253	27	6	McMurray
20	Powers, Warren	DB	6-0	190	27	6	Nebraska
79	Schuh, Harry	OT	6-2	260	25	4	Memphis State
76	Svihus, Bob	OT	6-4	245	24	4	Southern California
22	Todd, Larry	OE	6-1	185	25	4	Arizona State
63	Upshaw, Eugene	G-T	6-5	255	22	2	Texas A&I
38	Warner, Charlie	DB	6-0	170	28	5	Prairie View A&M
81	Wells, Warren	OE	6-1	190	25	3	Texas Southern
29	Williams, Howie	DB	6-1	186	31	7	Howard
52	Williamson, John	LB	6-2	220	25	5	Louisiana Tech

OAKLAND RAIDERS   1968 Top Rookies

NAME	POS.	HT.	WT.	AGE	COLLEGE	HOW ACQUIRED*
Dickey, Eldridge	O B	6-2	198	22	Tennessee A&I	D-1
Harper, John	G	6-2	250	22	Adams State	D-7
Shell, Arthur	OT	6-5	265	21	Maryland State	D-3
Smith, Charles	O B	6-2	200	22	Utah	D-4
Stabler, Ken	Q B	6-2	194	21	Alabama	D-2

*D — Draft (Number indicates draft round)
FA — Free Agent

OAKLAND RAIDERS   1968 Schedule

Sept. 15 — at Buffalo	1:30	Nov. 3 — Kansas City	1:00
Sept. 21 — at Miami	8:00	Nov. 10 — at Denver	1:00
Sept. 29 — at Houston	3:00	Nov. 17 — New York	1:00
Oct. 6 — Boston	1:00	Nov. 24 — at Cincinnati	1:30
Oct. 13 — San Diego	1:00	Nov. 28 — Buffalo	1:00
Oct. 20 — at Kansas City	3:00	Dec. 8 — Denver	1:00
Oct. 27 — Cincinnati	1:00	Dec. 15 — at San Diego	1:00

SAN DIEGO CHARGERS

San Diego Charger head coach Sid Gillman has made a career of building great offenses, and the one he now possesses is one of the most explosive he's ever put together.

It starts with super-star Lance Alworth at flanker, and runs through an offensive line that is one of the best at protecting a quarterback, in this case, John Hadl.

Last year that line, made up of Ron Mix and Ernie Wright at tackles, Sam Grueneisen at center, and Walt Sweeney and Gary Kirner at guards, only allowed Hadl to be dropped 11 times during the entire season. They also combined to open holes for one of the game's most consistent running attacks. This year, Wright is missing (gone to Cincinnati) but 6 foot 7 inch Terry Owens has more than adequately taken up the slack.

Quarterback John Hadl is the key to the Chargers' point production, and he has three of the finest receivers in the AFL. Lance Alworth can do anything from his flanker position, but he has two especially good moves that complement each other. The first is the down-and-in, then the takeoff, the zig-out.

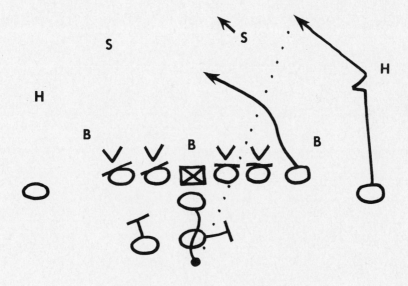

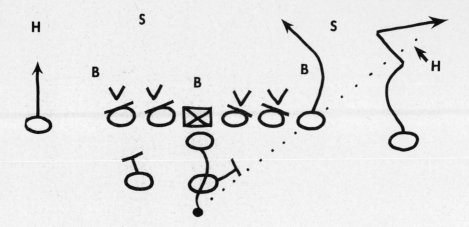

At tight end, another of Hadl's receivers is Willie Frazier. Willie caught 57 passes last year, as well as contributing mightily to the Chargers' running game. Frazier is seldom double-covered, because most defensive teams play to stop Alworth and consequently leave Frazier covered only by the tight safety.

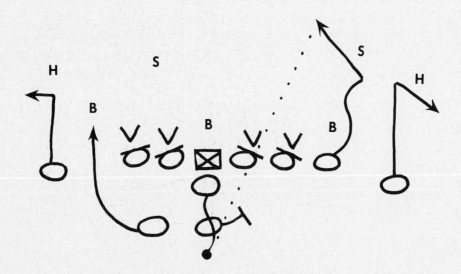

While quarterback John Hadl is a fine runner and scrambler himself, he has some of the game's best at his beck and call. Last year, when such outstanding veterans as Paul Lowe and Gene Foster were injured, Dick Post (known as Mighty Mouse—he's 5 feet 9 inches and 190 pounds) and Brad Hubbert moved in and divided 1,200 yards between them. Post and Lowe are the men to watch on the sweep, which Hadl likes to run on first and ten or third and short.

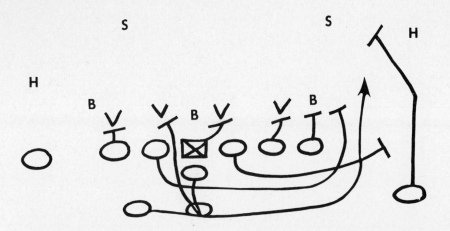

Defensively is where the Chargers must shape up if they are going to win an AFL title. While last year they were fairly effective in stopping the opposition's running game, they almost totally lacked a good pass rush. This year keep an eye on rookie Russ Washington. He's huge at 6 feet 6 inches and 290 pounds, and Sid Gillman picked him in the draft to do one thing, pressure the opposition's quarterback.

At linebacker, the Chargers are just adequate, and the big question is whether middle man Rick Redman will continue to develop in the middle.

The Chargers will also be undergoing some changes in their secondary this year. The first one has already been made, Chuck Weber being hired away from Boston to coach and concentrate on that one department. Speedy Duncan is possibly the only stick-out among the Chargers' pass defenders, but the entire unit could be strengthened if former All-League safety man Kenny Graham can bounce back from an injury-plagued 1967.

In summation, the Chargers are a fun team to watch that will have to show dramatic improvement on defense if they are going to make it to the play-off.

They have it all on defense, and for sheer enjoyment watch Lance Alworth cut up pass defenders with the best variety of moves in football.

SAN DIEGO CHARGERS   1968 Veterans Roster

NO.	NAME	POS.	HT.	WT.	AGE	YRS. IN PRO	COLLEGE
71	Akin, Harold	T	6-5	260	23	2	Oklahoma State
50	Allen, Chuck	LB	6-0	225	29	8	Washington
32	Allison, Jim	HB	6-0	215	24	4	San Diego State
19	Alworth, Lance	FLK	6-0	180	28	7	Arkansas
70	Appleton, Scott	DT	6-3	270	24	5	Texas
63	Asmond, Bob	G	6-1	265	24	R	N. Carolina College
84	Baker, John	LB	6-3	238	26	6	Mississippi State
40	Beauchamp, Joe	DB	5-11	185	23	3	Iowa State
86	Billingsley, Ron	DE	6-7	265	23	2	Wyoming
68	Briggs, Bob	DT	6-4	280	23	R	Heidelberg

NO.	NAME	POS.	HT.	WT.	AGE	YRS. IN PRO	COLLEGE
31	Brittenum, Jon	QB-DB	6-0	185	24	R	Arkansas
44	Cordill, Olie	E	6-1	181	24	2	Memphis State
88	Day, Tom	DE	6-2	262	33	8	N. Carolina A&T
82	DeLong, Steve	DE	6-2	252	25	4	Tennessee
45	Duncan, Leslie	DB	5-10	175	25	5	Jackson State
62	Erickson, Bernard	LB	6-1	235	23	2	Abilene Christian
37	Foster, Gene	FB	5-11	220	25	4	Arizona State
83	Frazier, Willie	E	6-4	225	25	5	Arkansas AM&N
27	Garrison, Gary	E	6-1	195	23	3	San Diego State
33	Graham, Kenny	DB	6-0	195	26	5	Washington State
79	Gross, George	DT	6-3	270	27	6	Auburn
65	Gruneisen, Sam	C	6-1	250	27	7	Villanova
21	Hadl, John	QB	6-1	215	28	7	Kansas
24	Howard, Bob	DB	6-2	190	23	2	San Diego State
26	Hubbert, Brad	FB	6-0	227	27	2	Arizona
72	Kirner, Gary	G	6-3	255	26	5	Southern California
73	Little, Larry	G	6-1	270	22	2	Bethune-Cookman
23	Lowe, Paul	HB	6-0	205	31	9	Oregon State
38	MacKinnon, Jacque	E	6-4	250	29	8	Colgate
74	Mix, Ron	T	6-4	250	30	9	Southern California
25	Newell, Steve	E	6-1	186	23	2	Long Beach State
76	Owens, Terry	T	6-6	250	23	3	Jacksonville State
22	Post, Dick	HB	5-9	191	22	2	Houston
57	Print, Bob	LB	6-0	220	24	2	Dayton
66	Redman, Rick	LB	6-0	225	25	4	Washington
80	Ridge, Houston	DT	6-4	245	23	3	San Diego State
20	Smith, Russ	HB	6-0	209	23	2	Miami (Fla.)
81	Staggs, Jeff	LB	6-2	248	24	2	San Diego State
18	Stephenson, Kay	QB	6-1	210	23	2	Florida
78	Sweeney, Walt	G	6-3	255	27	6	Syracuse
43	Tolbert, Jim	DB	6-3	207	24	3	Lincoln
47	Whitehead, Bud	DB	5-11	185	29	8	Florida State
41	Whitmyer, Nat	DB	5-11	180	27	3	Washington

SAN DIEGO CHARGERS   1968 Top Rookies

NAME	POS.	HT.	WT.	AGE	COLLEGE	HOW ACQUIRED*
Dyer, Ken	FL	6-3	185	22	Arizona State	D-4
Fenner, Lane	FL	6-5	207	23	Florida State	D-7
Hill, James	DB	6-2	192	22	Texas A&I	D-1a
Lenkaitis, William	C	6-3	250	22	Penn State	D-2
Perry, William	TE	6-2	220	23	Kent State	D-5
Washington, Russ	T	6-6	280	22	Missouri	D-1

*D— Draft (Number indicates draft round)
FA— Free Agent

SAN DIEGO CHARGERS   1968 Schedule

Sept. 9 — Cincinnati	6:00		Nov. 3 — Miami	1:00
Sept. 22 — Houston	1:00		Nov. 10 — at Boston	1:30
Sept. 29 — at Cincinnati	1:30		Nov. 17 — at Buffalo	1:30
Oct. 5 — at New York	8:00		Nov. 24 — New York	1:00
Oct. 13 — at Oakland	1:00		Dec. 1 — at Denver	2:00
Oct. 20 — Denver	1:00		Dec. 8 — Kansas City	1:00
Oct. 27 — at Kansas City	3:00		Dec. 15 — Oakland	1:00

HOW TO WATCH THE GAME

People have been asking me for years how to watch the game of professional football. I have rather a stock answer to that question. However, when I give it, I usually get a quizzical, "come on, you're putting me on" look. The answer, which apparently isn't sophisticated enough, is to follow the ball.

A lot of pro football fans take away from their own pleasure in viewing a game by looking for elements that are but a tiny part of the whole. Oh, I suppose that the real astute fan can get a kick out of watching the footwork of a defensive back or the work of a particularly good offensive tackle or guard, but the game really takes place around the ball.

What I try to do in watching a game is play it mentally myself. I try to know the teams as well as possible and their particular personality or approach to the game.

As I've said earlier, there are only a few situations that occur with any frequency in football. They are again: first and ten, second and short (one to four yards), second and long (five yards plus), third and short (one to three yards), third and long (four yards plus), and the various fourth-down situations that are influenced by score, time remaining, field position, and other factors.

All teams go into a game with a game plan. They have determined from a week-long study of their opponent that in each situation, a certain defense is best, or a certain offensive play will be more effective. The results of these studies are known as "frequencies," or more simply put, the percentage of times a team will do a certain thing in a given situation.

These frequencies also help the football fan watch a football game. If, for instance, you're watching Cleveland play Dallas, keep a mental account of what plays the offensive teams like to run in as many of the situations as you can.

As the game progresses, you'll be surprised how many times each team will use the same play every time they are confronted with the same situation. It won't be long into the game before you can say to yourself, it's third and eight, Ryan will probably be going to Collins on that down-and-in, or Morin over the middle on the turn-in.

After you've established your own frequency, it is now time to watch the specialty of the game. If you're a Dallas fan, chances are you'll want to watch Cornell Green, the Cowboy defensive corner back, to see how he covers Collins. By the same token, if you're a Browns fan, you'll probably want to watch either Collins run his pattern or Ryan's pass protection.

Many times you'll be taken by surprise, because both the defensive and offensive quarterbacks are aware of the other's knowledge of their team, and consequently they will sometimes break up their frequency. However, you'll be right more than you'll be wrong, because the reason each team has a frequency of doing a certain thing on a certain situation is because that's what they do best.

There are, of course, many other "keys" to watching pro football. Some of them are: If you think a team might be planning a red-dog, watch the free safety. Just before the ball is snapped, if he moves up closer to the line of scrimmage than he has been playing, chances are your suspicions are correct. He does this because he knows that with the linebacker red-dogging, he must now be in a position to take the linebacker's man.

Watch the corner back when you think a defensive secondary is going to double-cover a certain receiver. If he starts up closer to the line of scrimmage before the ball is snapped, chances are he is going to cover short and the safety will come over and cover deep.

If you're having trouble following the ball on running plays, you can generally watch the guards, as they more than likely will be leading any play that goes to the outside, or driving to the hole if the play is hitting inside.

If a team begins to use a lot of double flankers, they generally are doing this to ensure that they will get man-to-man coverage in the secondary. At this time, you usually can determine who the offensive team considers the weak link in a defensive secondary, because that's the man they will attempt to beat.

Many times you can determine if a quarterback is going to call a pass play or a run simply by noticing the amount of time spent in the huddle. A pass play will take longer to call than a running play in most instances. The reason is simple: there is just more for the quarterback to say. For instance, a pass play might be called flanker right, 1 X right, L split seven, A and B circle. And then too there might be some quick comment by the receivers, such as, "I'll take it down ten before I break it off," etc.

In contrast to the pass play, most running plays are simple and quickly defined. A running play might merely require the following call: flanker right 36-slant. Many quarterbacks try to compensate for the time differential, but in the heat of a game, or when time is running out, they either forget, or can't afford the luxury.

Watch the quarterback at the line of scrimmage, looking over the defense. He generally has set automatics he calls against certain defenses. It is often obvious that he is changing the play at the line of scrimmage. If you think he is, try and recognize the defense and make a mental note of the situation and the play he calls. The next time that same situation presents itself, and you see the quarterback obviously changing the play, you'll have a good idea of where he is going.

Watch the activities on the bench if you have the opportunity. Many times you'll see a quarterback and a receiver in a heated discussion while the defense is on the field, and it's surprising how many times on the next offensive series the quarterback will team with that receiver on a pass.

These are a few of the things I look for, and of course there are many more. But, again, the best way to watch a game is to know the two teams involved. Each and every team has a personality, and it seldom changes. And each and every player has certain things he does best. Consequently, that's what you can expect most.

OFFICIATING

The National Football League, with 16 teams in action this fall, will employ 51 men for the purpose of officiating. These 51 men, 90 percent of whom have had experience as players, are divided into eight working teams of six men each, with three men available as swing men in case of illness, injury, etc.

To become an NFL official, you don't merely turn in your player's helmet for a set of stripes. Applicants are screened and scrutinized by Mark Duncan, the NFL's Supervisor of Officials, who is headquartered in the NFL office in New York City.

When an applicant is selected, he must first meet some rather stiff requirements, off the field as well as on. All of today's officials are independently employed outside of football. Numbered among today's active officials are lawyers, high school principals, school teachers, and successful businessmen from many walks of life.

After one is accepted as an official he attends a special school conducted by the NFL and presided over by Mark Duncan. This special session takes place in July, lasts five days, and both the newly initiated and the veteran officials are required to be present. Hours are spent viewing films of previous games in which rule infractions have occurred. Key situations are set up theoretically, and the students render their decisions.

They spend additional hours discussing what may have been trends toward dominant infractions during the previous year, and they also discuss the many unforseeable elements that in six months could have a major bearing on the outcome of a ball game, such as the inevitable dog on the field, a suddenly deflated football, or a disgruntled fan attempting to invade the huddle.

They also work on the field, illustrating to each other infractions that can occur, and conditioning themselves much as do the ball players for the months ahead.

Their pay as officials ranges upward from $1800 a year, the minimum annual guarantee. Each official receives against that guarantee $250 for each game he works (after five years this goes to $300.) There are special games, such as the Championship and Super Bowl, in which the base fee goes as high as $1,000.

While this extra money is certainly attractive, over the years I have found that most of the officials consider their secondary profession a labor of love, rather than an economic necessity.

To my way of thinking, they do a superb job under sometimes almost impossible conditions. In the heat of a game, they must remain cool and detached, rendering judgments and decisions as objectively as King Solomon. They are often the object of abuse from fans, coaches, players and the wives of all; yet they do their job, rising above all this, and they do it extremely well.

I have often answered a Monday morning quarterback's criticism of an official with a question: "How would you like to have made that same call?"

OFFICIALS' SIGNALS

Crawling, Pushing, or Helping Runner
PENALTY — FIVE YARDS. Also used when offense uses flying wedge or interlocked blocking — PENALTY — FIFTEEN YARDS.

Dead Ball
Play has stopped. When fist is closed, it is signal for fourth down.

Delay of Game
Also indicates an excessive request for a time-out. Signal followed by circular motion of a referee's forearms indicates an illegal formation. PENALTY — FIVE YARDS.

First Down
Arm swung in direction of first down.

Holding or Illegal Use of Hands
PENALTY — FOR OFFENSE, FIFTEEN YARDS: FOR DEFENSE, FIVE YARDS.

Illegal Forward Pass
More than one forward pass in one offensive play, or pass has been thrown by player beyond line of scrimmage. PENALTY— FIVE YARDS. Signal also used for deliberately grounding ball. PENALTY — FIFTEEN YARDS.

Illegal Motion At Snap
All offensive players, except one backfield man, must remain motionless until snap. Man in motion can only move parallel to line, or away from it. Linemen whose movements may draw a member of the opposition offside, are also vulnerable to this call. PENALTY—FIVE YARDS.

Interference
A player has prevented another from catching or intercepting a pass—PENALTY —OFFENSE LOSES DOWN AND FIFTEEN YARDS FROM POINT OF PLAY; DEFENSE YIELDS A FIRST DOWN AT POINT OF FOUL.
Also applies when a punt receiver has signalled for a fair catch and he or the reception is interfered with. PENALTY — FIFTEEN YARDS.

Loss of Down
Team guilty of infraction loses down.

Offside
Offensive or defensive linemen have crossed line of scrimmage before snap.

Penalty Refused,
Incompleted Pass,
Missed Field Goal
or Extra Point, or Play Over
Indicates that fouled team has refused penalty and will accept previous play. Also that play has failed.

Personal Foul
Unnecessary roughness. Followed by swing of leg, indicates roughing-the-kicker, followed by forward motion of raised arm, indicates roughing-the-passer, and followed by chopping motion at leg, indicates clipping. PENALTY — FIFTEEN YARDS.

Safety
Ball is dead in offensive team's end zone, while it is in team's possession (ball carrier tackled behind goal line). Defense is awarded two points.

Time-In
Signal to start the clock. Also indicates that there is no time-out, play continues.

Time-Out
Signal automatically stops clock. Followed by one arm swung at side, signal indicated touchback. When referee places one hand on cap, it indicates he has called time-out, and neither team will be charged.

Touchdown, Field Goal or Conversion
A team has scored.

Unsportsmanlike Conduct
For an "act which is contrary to the generally understood principles of sportsmanship"—abusive action or gestures toward opponents or officials or action tending to disrupt game. PENALTY — FIFTEEN YARDS.

ABOUT THE AUTHOR

Frank Gifford, CBS Sports Broadcaster and color analyst of all New York Giants and other NFL telecasts, was for twelve years a star back with the Giants —six times an All-Pro and the NFL's Most Valuable Player in 1956. An All-American at the University of Southern California, he joined the Giants in 1952. When he retired in March, 1965, he had accumulated the phenomenal record of 484 points scored, 78 touchdowns including 35 by rushing, 367 pass receptions for 5,484 yards, and 3,704 yards on the ground. In addition to his network duties on football telecasts, Frank is Sports Director of WCBS-TV in New York and anchor man on CBS Radio's nightly "Worldwide Sports."